FINEGAN KRUCKEMEYER has had 101 plays performed on six continents and in eight languages. His work has enjoyed seasons in over 200 international festivals and in 2018, he was the most-produced playwright of original children's theatre in the US. His work has received 42 awards, including the Mickey Miners Lifetime Achievement Award for international Theatre for Young Audiences, David Williamson Prize for Excellence in Australian Playwrighting, seven Australian Writers Guild Awards and an inaugural Sidney Myer Fellowship. He has spoken at conferences in ten countries, with papers published and works studied at many international universities. Finegan was born in Ireland and moved halfway around the world to Adelaide aged eight. After 15 years, he and his wife Essie left for the island state of Tasmania. And after 15 more, with their son Moe, they returned.

www.finegankruckemeyer.com

Ansuya Nathan in the STCSA production of HIBERNATION. *(Photo: Matt Byrne)*

HIBERNATION

Finegan Kruckemeyer

CURRENCY PRESS
The performing arts publisher

CURRENCY PLAYS

First published in 2022
by Currency Press Pty Ltd,
PO Box 2287, Strawberry Hills, NSW, 2012, Australia
enquiries@currency.com.au
www.currency.com.au

Typeset by Brighton Gray for Currency Press.
Cover design by Andy Ellis for Currency Press.

Contents

Currency Press acknowledges the Traditional Owners of the Country on which we live and work. We pay our respects to all Aboriginal and Torres Strait Islander Elders, past and present.

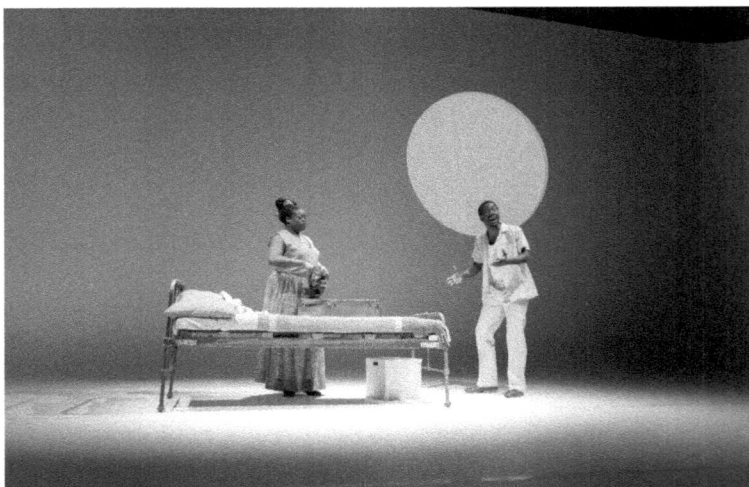

Kialea-Nadine Williams and Rashidi Edward in the STCSA production of HIBERNATION. *(Photo: Matt Byrne)*

Introduction

Can art, can theatre effect social change? Did *The Crucible* contribute to the end of McCarthyism? *Master Harold ... and the boys* apartheid? *Top Girls* Thatcherism? Does a play like *Angels in America* combat homophobia?

Maybe. Maybe not. But I reckon it helps.

What theatre can do, without question, is offer a fresh perspective. Imagination can activate a part of our brain that data cannot.

And despite the lobbying efforts of the fossil fuel industry and its plutocrats, the data and science on climate change is clear.

In the next few years, according to the UN's Intergovernmental Panel on Climate Change, we can either hope for strong participation in all major world regions in a phase out of internal combustion vehicles, a scale-up in sourcing bioenergy—for carbon capture and storage, ecosystem-based economic practices, large-scale reforestation, plant-based diets and cities where life is intertwined with nature, not separate from it. Or with no participation and no regulation or price on carbon emissions, we will see more drought, stress on water resources, unviable agriculture, major conflicts, extreme weather events, species extinction, decreased biodiversity, rapid sea-level rise and coastal inundation, fragmented global communities and a substantial reduction in humanity's health and wellbeing.

Eric Holthaus writes in *The Future Earth: A Radical Vision for What's Possible in the Age of Warming*, 'our futures are simultaneously dependent on the actions of others and defined by our personal daily choices. This reality demands that we interact with one another, that we come together—for our own survival and the survival of life as we know it on our planet'.

While Michael E. Mann in *The Climate War* posits: 'Personal actions, from going vegan to avoiding flying, are increasingly touted as the primary solution to the climate crisis. Though these actions are worth taking, a fixation on voluntary action alone takes the pressure off the push for governmental policies to hold corporate polluters accountable.'

It's a problem for all of us, individuals and governments alike.

We need systemic change, we need to educate the confused, we need to disregard the doomsayers but most of all, we need to question that which has led to the problem.

Finegan's bold and brilliant play began as an idea with which I was immediately captured. It questions the very nature of our industrialised world and the need to consume at all costs. What happens when industry gets paused, when nothing is consumed?

Finegan wondered what impact a globally sanctioned shutdown would have (and this was months before a thing called Covid-19 existed). And wondered how we connect to ourselves and to others in the midst of such great change.

Any theatre company worth its salt in this period of history in which we find ourselves should be wrestling with how it can activate works that explore and encourage the need for climate change action. In Finegan's idea, I knew I'd found a unique exploration of that very thing.

At the time Finegan presented his initial idea for the play over a coffee, our company's commission budget was tied up on other projects but I was hopeful that he would see my genuine enthusiasm for his idea and start writing in any case! What then followed was my awakening to what a prolific, fast, open-minded and genius artist he is. Within several months, he sent me a first act that I read on my phone while backstage during a rather long tech rehearsal session on another play I was working on in Sydney. I was gobsmacked and delighted by its ambition, its flow, its wit, its marriage of suspenseful narrative and poetic scope, its characters—flawed, human, reaching—and its truly global nature. The speech that ended Act One in which the elements of the sleeping world are listed took my breath away (and it remains mostly unchanged now from that first draft). I mouthed a silent 'wow' and knew immediately that this work needed to be seen.

Within days of this backstage reading, Covid-19 hit. Suddenly, this page 12 news item had crept to the front page and the world was about to be very different. The play I was working on in Sydney was cancelled, I had to hurry back to Adelaide before borders shut and into lockdown we all went.

Theatres closed, traffic stopped, the world waited. The sleeping world Finegan had imagined no longer seemed so distant a possibility.

Soon, I was able to squirrel away some commission money and I urged Finegan to continue with the play, now as a full commission for us. He talked of an Act Two where the world wakes from its hibernation and ponders its future. I couldn't wait to see what he'd deliver. But I also threw him a curve ball. I wondered what would happen before the slumber was over. Did everyone sleep? And from there, Finegan then posited more questions. Were there glitches in the system? And what would happen if there were? What if a handful of people didn't fall into sleep, following the world governments' activation of that hibernation? (I won't spoil for you how that occurs in the play!)

Finegan embraced this idea and set to work.

I also encouraged him to do the opposite of what many directors and dramaturgs do. I dared him to expand rather than edit. Make it longer. Explore all the tangents. Colour in as much as possible rather than minimise. It felt like we had the keys to the secret garden and now was the time to go wherever we wanted with the work.

And then his bravery, courage and humility as an artist came into even clearer focus for me as he dived deeper into this pool of possibilities.

What resulted was a middle act very different in structure, tone and tempo to the first act. And by allowing us to focus on two characters in a sea of others, he offered the micro within the macro to fantastic effect. And this in turn provided an emotional well from which the themes in Act Three, particularly those about change, choice and forgiveness, could truly spring.

I'm so grateful to him for the initial idea, for the play that evolved (and his smart and gracious collaboration throughout), for the platform it gave for a wonderful cast and creative team to unleash their breathtaking talents and for creating a work that led to every single one of us at State Theatre Company South Australia to notch up our own climate action knowledge and efforts. I know it has inspired our audiences and will inspire many others to similar reflection, regeneration and action.

I'm sure Finegan would join me in thanking the many scientists, environmentalists and activists who assisted in the creation of this work too. They are heroes. Here's hoping that we can all approach this crisis as heroically and as quickly as possible.

Mitchell Butel
Adelaide, December 2021

Mitchell Butel is a director and actor. He is Artistic Director of State Theatre Company South Australia, and directed the world premiere production of *Hibernation* at STCSA.

Hibernation was first performed by the State Theatre Company of South Australia at the Dunstan Playhouse, Adelaide Festival Centre, on 13 August 2021, with the following cast:

PETE / SANG	James Smith
MAGGIE	Elizabeth Hay
EMILY METCALFE	Ansuya Nathan
WARWICK GRANT	Mark Saturno
DAMIAN ACCUARDI / LUIS FLORES / CUSTOMS OFFICIAL	Chris Asimos
MARK OBRECHT / ERNESTO FLORES / CUSTOMS OFFICIAL	Ezra Juanta
KELLY KNOWLES / CHIDERA OKOYE	Kialea-Nadine Williams
AZIBUIKE OKOYE / NIGEL	Rashidi Edward
CASSANDRA FLORES / ALEX HALL	Rosalba Clemente
JEONG	Eva Hinde and Poppy Kelly
SPEAKER OF THE HOUSE / MINISTERS	Ensemble

Director and Dramaturg, Mitchell Butel
Assistant Director, Clement Rukundo
Designer, Jonathon Oxlade
Associate Costume Designer, Ailsa Paterson
Lighting Designer, Gavin Norris
Video Designer, Matt Byrne
Sound Designer and Composer, Andrew Howard
Additional Composition, Nate Edmondson

For Moe, and Lila and Ivy and Malachi and Hattie,
and all those who must pick up what we have dropped

CHARACTERS

Canberra, Australia
WARWICK GRANT
DAMIAN ACCUARDI
EMILY METCALFE
MARK OBRECHT
OPPOSITION MINISTERS
GOVERNMENT MINISTERS
SPEAKER OF THE HOUSE
NIGEL

Los Angeles, USA
KELLY KNOWLES
ALEX HALL

Lagos, Nigeria
CHIDERA OKOYE
AZUBUIKE OKOYE

Seoul, South Korea
JEONG
SANG
CUSTOMS OFFICIALS 1 and 2

Bogota, Colombia
CASSANDRA FLORES
ERNESTO FLORES
LUIS FLORES

Adelaide, Australia
PETE
MAGGIE

NOTES

1. Act Two takes place in the city or town where your production occurs, so as to provide the audience with the sensation of a familiar environment beset by an unfamiliar event. As such, the name of a river, a mall and some streets must be localised (these street names are referenced again in Act Three). Such edits may be undertaken by the company and simply require approval from the writer.

2. Doubling of casting is at the discretion of the company, director and performers, so as to best accommodate your ensemble's needs. What is imperative, however, is the Prologue's descriptor: 'an ensemble denoting a globe populates the space, culturally and physiologically diverse'. This allusion to broad demographics must be present—and ideally seen also in Act Two's casting, so as not to centre an Anglo story in what is a global exercise.

From left: Rashidi Edward, Ezra Juanta and Mark Saturno in the STCSA production of HIBERNATION. (Photo: Matt Byrne)

ACT ONE

PROLOGUE

The stage is full of furniture—chairs, desks, beds, couches, tables etc—denoting culturally and socio-economically diverse environments.

The configurations suggest various domestic and professional settings—a lounge, a dining table, an office, a senate chamber etc. However, all these environments seem haphazardly overlaid, furniture from one room / culture / context close to or encroaching upon another.

An ensemble denoting a globe populates the space, culturally and physiologically diverse.

SCENE ONE (H-18 MONTHS)

WARWICK GRANT *sits at an expensive desk, poring over the paperwork heaped upon it. A polite knock and* DAMIAN ACCUARDI *enters.* WARWICK *remains focussed on his work.*

DAMIAN: Minister?

WARWICK: Damian. You good?

DAMIAN: Yes thanks. If that's okay I'd just /

WARWICK: / Sure the press conference is still set for two?

DAMIAN: Yeah it's all ready. Liste /

WARWICK: / 'Cause Henry Lau is a fucking snake. We blink, he'll run his own one at midday, say it was all China's idea and forget to mention us.

DAMIAN: It's all set.

WARWICK: You mark my words.

DAMIAN: Marked. Listen, I have Emily Metcalfe here.

> *He nods to her offstage and she enters tentatively.*

WARWICK: [*glancing up*] Okay?

DAMIAN: Emily works for you—research and on policy language.

WARWICK: Well … fine. Thanks, Em. Listen I have a shitload of /

DAMIAN: / Emily has an idea.

WARWICK *pauses in his studying of the papers.*

WARWICK: So discuss it with the relevant department, guys. There's a process to this shit you know.

DAMIAN: I know, Minis /

WARWICK: / I'm launching thirteen billion in joint space funding in … [*Consulting his watch*] Four and a half hours (Jesus Christ …) so unless Natalie's idea is /

EMILY: / Emily.

WARWICK: I … really don't give a shit, darling. Actually you know what, I kind of do now but not in the way you were hoping. Both of you back it up, shut the door behind you. Fuck's sake …

DAMIAN: Warwick.

WARWICK: 'Minister' …

DAMIAN *doesn't give.*

What?

DAMIAN: I am your policy man.

WARWICK: You are for the moment yeah …

DAMIAN: And Emily has come up with what I believe is some *very good* policy.

WARWICK: Come up with? What's that mean? You guys been working on this?

EMILY *looks to* DAMIAN *who gestures for her to go ahead.*

EMILY: No. I thought of it at home.

WARWICK: Oh and she's brought it in to share? Yeah no I've got time for show and tell, that's great. Hang on, where's that go-kart I built with my dad?

DAMIAN: Minister.

WARWICK: I've got China arriving in three hours!

DAMIAN: This is bigger than China!

Beat.

Say it, Emily.

WARWICK: Say it quickly, Emily.

EMILY: Yes! Okay! As minister for space exploration, you look at off-planet sites for the benefit of humankind. We need a fallback soon and … Mars potentially offers that.

WARWICK: Fucking hope you write my policy better than you talk it …
EMILY: But! I think I've found a planet which *will* satisfy all our needs.

He shows interest.

And … instead of doing everything we can to reach it, I propose …
we do nothing we can.

WARWICK: [*to* DAMIAN] What. The fuck?
EMILY: [*more urgently*] I think the … *doing*'s been our mistake, Minister.
We're throwing *billions* at a space race clouded by everyone aiming
at a different thing. So: we stop that. We introduce a single policy.

She places a document on his desk, and he scans it.

You introduce a single policy. And the world gets behind it.

WARWICK: [*still reading*] You're saying Australia just fucks off a China
treaty I spent three years building. Why would I do that?
EMILY: Because Minister … 'Henry Lau is a fucking snake. We blink,
and he'll say it was all China's idea and forget to mention us.'

He looks at her.

With this … [*Referencing the document*] You forget to mention him.

WARWICK: And why would anyone listen? What stops us getting locked
out of every chat, with every country, from here on in?
DAMIAN: 'Cause it's good. It's different and big-concept but … Yeah
it's good.

WARWICK: [*looking up from the pages*] You wrote this?

EMILY *nods.*

What'd you say your name was again?
EMILY: Emily Metcalfe, Sir.

He lays the document down on his desk and looks at them both.

WARWICK: Fucking hell …
DAMIAN: Absolutely, Sir.

SCENE TWO (H-17 MONTHS)

US breakfast TV anchors ALEX HALL *and* KELLY KNOWLES *sit at a
shared desk, looking serious.*

KELLY: Sadly, all three of the pandas … had to be euthanised.

Both look even more stoic.

A truly sad story there.

ALEX: Absolutely, Kelly. It seems sometimes, things really are just black and whi /

KELLY *does a small cough signalling* ALEX *to stop.*

But in lighter news!

Both snap into smiling states.

We're getting reports of some interesting viewing from our friends in Australia.

KELLY: Good-dye, mates!

ALEX: [*laughing*] Kelly—you do that really well!

KELLY: I might have had an *Aussie* boyfriend or two in college.

ALEX: Of course you did.

KELLY: … ?

ALEX: So it seems a TV show over there got some wild ratings. And that show … was 'Parliamentary Question Time'!

KELLY: Are you serious, Alex?

ALEX: That's what it says on my screen. It seems this guy—he's called Warwick Grant and he's their minister for space exploration.

KELLY: Huh.

ALEX: So a speech he made back on Tuesday was tuned into by a massive *41 percent* of the good folks down under.

KELLY: I'll take those ratings!

ALEX: Me too—make mine a double!

KELLY: [*laughing and making a drinking mime*] Bet you've said that a few times, Alex.

ALEX: … ?

KELLY: So how's *Aussie* Question Time work then? Was the question: 'Ah, shall we throw another shrimp on the barby?!'

Both laugh uproariously.

ALEX: Good one! 'Er, shall we vote which animal is gonna kill us today?!'

More laughter.

ALEX: 'Shall we raise hands if we *didn't* go out with Kelly in colle' /

KELLY: [*seriously*] / Just leave it /

ALEX: / Sure. [*Checking her papers*] Here's a clip of the speech from, ah … Minister Grant.

> WARWICK *rises from a new chair and stands, addressing the House. Other ensemble members sit in various chairs as government or opposition parliamentarians. Support from his own party and jeers from the opposition are heard throughout.*

WARWICK: We are finding ourselves at a *catastrophic* moment in time!

OPP: Good on the government for finally admitting it!

> *The opposition roars with laughter.* WARWICK *is not fazed.*

WARWICK: And by we, I mean everyone. Everyone is the victim of what is happening to our planet. And, though not popular to admit, *everyone is the culprit* for what is happening to our planet.

> *A chorus of support and opposition.*

Yes, my colleagues across the aisle can shake their heads—ignoring the truth is what they have always done! And will continue to do!

> *Roars.*

But! It is not about them. Or us. It is about Australia! It is about the world!

Mass food shortages since '26! Nine nation states already submerged and their populations now … wreaking havoc on every border we hold sacred!

OPP: They are dying!

WARWICK: Oh dying to get in here you mean?! Absolutely they are, Member for Ross. And what do they find if your lot let them in? A Murray-Darling water table down to its last drops! New ghost towns created each week! Vast tracts of farmland that can't hold enough topsoil to grow a bloody thing!

The world is sick—and we need a cure!

OPP: You've forgotten your portfolio, mate! You're space exploration, not health.

> *Roars.*

SPEAKER: Order! Order I say!

WARWICK: Thank you, Madam Speaker. Yes, Member for Lockley, I am the federal minister for space exploration. Along with my global colleagues, I am given the *great honour* of working with the *great minds*.

OPP: Where are they then!?

WARWICK: Of working with the *great* scientific minds to explore the reaches of space! To find landforms which'll sustain human life long after I am gone and, much as it pains me to say it, long after that lot are gone as well!

PRO: Yes Minister!

WARWICK: And we have done it!

PRO: Yes we have!

OPP: Bullshit!

SPEAKER: Order! The Member for Sutton is ejected from the chamber!

WARWICK: We have done it, I say! [*Beat*] There is a planet for us, *and* our children, *and* their children. It has been staring us in the face all along! And instead of doing *everything* we can to make our survival a reality … We must do *nothing* we can!

OPP: He's finally cracked.

Laughter.

WARWICK: The answer, Madam Speaker, the very simple answer, to this very complex problem … is 54E.

A crescendo of noise from all sides ensues, the parliament dispersing.

SCENE THREE (H-SIX MONTHS)

CHIDERA OKOYE *is packing a bag which lies open on her bed. Her husband* AZUBUIKE *walks in.*

AZUBUIKE: What are you doing?

CHIDERA: Nothing.

AZUBUIKE: You're packing.

CHIDERA: … Okay.

AZUBUIKE: Why?

CHIDERA: For … for the year.

AZUBUIKE: But … [*Laughing*] Chide my sweetie-cocoa, we are not going anywhere. We are doing the exact opposite of going anywhere. We are about to have the most not-going-anywhere year of our lives.

CHIDERA: It's still …
AZUBUIKE: What?
CHIDERA: It's still a trip. It still feels like a trip.

Beat.

AZUBUIKE: It does. What did you pack?

He goes and looks in the suitcase.

Photos of the boys. Our letters. Aisha's slippers … [*Studying them, touched*] These are good things.
CHIDERA: I know they are.
AZUBUIKE: If you had packed a toothbrush or underpants, then I'd know you'd gone mad.
CHIDERA: Ah be quiet, old man.
AZUBUIKE: [*holding them up, laughing*] But you did pack our passports which are *very important* when you are travelling nowhere!
CHIDERA: Okay I'm happy you are making yourself happy.
AZUBUIKE: It's just funny!
CHIDERA: Yeah yeah …

Beat.

I have seen you too.
AZUBUIKE: What?
CHIDERA: You. Polishing your shoes. Polishing your shoes so nice and shiny—just so you can lie in bed in them.
AZUBUIKE: …
CHIDERA: We are not walking anywhere either. And no-one will be looking at our feet. So really, polishing shoes or packing passports … are as mad as each other.

Beat. He nods.

AZUBUIKE: It is in case I die. In case we all begin this. But we do not end it. Or we do not end it the way we meant to. [*Shrugging*] I want my shoes to look nice.

She smiles and hugs him.

CHIDERA: I know you do, my love. And I noticed as well.
AZUBUIKE: What?
CHIDERA: You have polished my shoes too. And the boys' shoes.

They are all as polished as each other.

Silence. He lets himself be held.

We do what we have to, Azubuike. We can all … only do that much.

SCENE FOUR (H-FOUR MONTHS)

SANG *sits on the floor with his daughter* JEONG, *as she lays down a train track which gradually extends around and beneath the legs of various pieces of furniture.*

JEONG: 54E is a strange name.

SANG: And that's just the start of it—the whole thing is: 54E-501E.

JEONG: How do you know all that?

SANG: I'm your dad. I know everything.

JEONG: No you don't.

SANG: [*nodding*] No I don't.

JEONG: Bo-Young's dad plays baseball and you don't even know the rules to baseball.

SANG: That's really true. Sorry, what I meant to say is: I know everything that's *actually important.*

> *She looks at him and he jokingly ignores her look, focussing on the track-building.*

What?

JEONG: That's rude.

SANG: You're right—sorry, Bo-Young's dad.

JEONG: But you're right too.

SANG: Am I? Great.

JEONG: Some things are more important than other things. At different times.

SANG: Wow—that's a huge thought, Jeong.

JEONG: Like, Bo-Young's dad does know all about baseball *but* ... he never remembers to pack her fruit for first recess.

SANG: [*shaking his head mock-disapprovingly*] Woah.

JEONG: And she said one time he *forgot* his wedding ring when he came home at night and her mum cried. Imagine forgetting your wedding ring?

SANG: Oh, Bo-Young's dad …

JEONG: And anyway, 54E is more important than baseball—that's actually my point.

SANG: Oh right. Well, yeah I agree. Baseball's fun but 54E-501E is maybe what'll save our whole world.

JEONG: How, Dad?

SANG: 'Cause … It'll make us like bears.

JEONG: I don't get it.

SANG: Well it's simple.

> JEONG *continues to lay the train track throughout the ensuing scenes.*

SCENE FIVE (H-18 MONTHS AND A DAY)

EMILY *sits across a restaurant table from* MARK OBRECHT.

EMILY: So … my department's space exploration. And there's a … consortium we're in—the G14. To find liveable places beyond Earth.

MARK: 'Cause we fucked it up?

EMILY: Basically. *Except* … There's this thing I've been … thinking about, just for the last week, like … Maybe we haven't?

MARK: We haven't fucked it up?

EMILY: Not completely. Like, a lot, yeah, don't get me wrong but …
Hang on, Mark—do I need to say 'off the record' or something?

MARK: [*laughing*] Nice of you to think but I'm such a fucking junior cadet it's not funny.

EMILY: …

MARK: [*seriously*] Honestly, Emily—I'm two months out of uni. The subeditor *I report to* thinks I'm called Mike. But sure—you're off the record.

EMILY: [*smiling*] 'Kay. Last week—it'd been a big day, fucked day. And I'm slumped on a couch. Drinking this. [*Lifting her glass*] Waiting to fall asleep basically. And I think of it. Falling asleep. [*Beat*] Do you know 54E?

MARK: Don't think so?

EMILY: Well … we've been focussed on Mars for a while now—if we need to start over.

MARK: How depressing.

EMILY: Oh it's a shithole. *But* it's a shithole that *could* sustain us. Only: it's a hundred and eighty days to get there. So a huge problem is ... [*Tapping her head*] This. Us as humans just ... not mentally equipped for half a year in a small pod. So we've had scientists, in labs, work on a solution. And then they found one: 54E-501E.

MARK: And what is it? What's it do?

EMILY: [*smiling*] It's hibernation.

MARK: For humans?!

EMILY: Yeah. It's a drug that ... switches you off basically. There's a physical suppressant—slows metabolism, halts your body's needs. A thermal thing for temperature.

And the bit I love: there's this mental stimulant, so you don't *realise* time's passing. It kind of ... massages your mind. Tells you a story, till you wake up.

MARK: Sounds amazing.

EMILY: Oh it's so clever. So beautiful I think.

MARK: So what? You send us off to space and we ... wake up somewhere and start again.

EMILY: No see that's the thing, Mark. That's what we think we've been working on—for years. Me too till ... last week. But then I'm lying there, so tired—so tired of *being* so tired, of losing sleep worrying what'll happen to us ... And I think:

Why not here? What if we all just climb into bed here? Shut the curtains, shut our eyes, take the drug ...

And hibernate.

MARK: And what's that do? We still wake up where we went to sleep.

EMILY: 'Cept we don't! Yeah geographically our bed's still our bed. But environmentally, ecologically, *one year later* ... we have no fucking idea what we wake up to.

MARK: What, like, vines climbing up buildings?

EMILY: Like: everything. Forest regeneration. Animal numbers. Oceans unfished for a year. Remember 2020?

MARK: Course. [*Beat*] My grandma died.

EMILY: Fuck. Sorry. I don't mean to /

MARK: / It's okay. A lot of people died.

She is more serious now.

EMILY: Well earlier, before … that. There were these reports coming in from Wuhan—from the first twenty-five days where they shut all its factories. And mostly they just talk about the money loss. *But alongside that* are these NASA images showing carbon dioxide levels *dropping*. Like, massively. And that's twenty-five days. With *three hundred and sixty-five* …

Anything could happen.

So that's what I've written in this big report that … [*Laughing*] no-one has asked me to write. That's what I'm putting on my boss' desk tomorrow morning. And, I don't know, maybe he does something with it. Maybe he shows it to *his* boss. Or maybe I'm fired. [*Laughing*] I have no idea.

MARK: I like it, Em, but … that *powerlessness*. Can we really just … close our eyes? Just let what happens … happen to us, for that long?

EMILY: Usually—no. But now—I think yes. I think we know this is a last chance.

SCENE SIX (H-17 MONTHS)

WARWICK *rises from a chair and addresses parliament. He is softer now, empathetic.*

WARWICK: A last chance.

A literal point of no return. Either we undertake this great leap of faith, here, in our own houses, in the places we know and love, among the people we know and love.

Beat.

Or we flee. We do what I and my colleagues worldwide have been setting in motion for years now, and we set our sights on new horizons, and start over. And I have no problem with this—it's what I've been elected to do. But.

He smiles and drops all formality.

As I sat at home in front of the telly last week. So tired. So tired of being so tired, of losing sleep worrying what'll happen to us … I found myself thinking not of distant solutions—but of nearby ones.

Beat. He smiles.

Of my kids, my wife asleep down the hall. My dog on his blanket. My coffee shop. My pub. The oval, just a block away, where we go watch the Blues do us proud.

He laughs a tired laugh.

And I thought: why not here? What if we all just ... climb into bed here? Shut the curtains, shut our eyes, take 54E ... And hibernate?

EMILY *has left the restaurant, and now packs a box, glaring at* WARWICK *as he orates.*

And yes—there are people far cleverer than me, who've come up with far cleverer solutions. But sometimes ... we don't need the cleverest answer.

We just need the right answer.

Some things are more important than other things. At different times. And at this time ... *This* is what's important. Here. Now. Saving what we know. What we love.

Prime Minister, Madam Speaker, colleagues with me, and across the aisle, friends with me, and across the globe ...

I ask you, for the good of all humanity—let's consider Hibernation.

EMILY *shakes her head and begins exiting, the box held in her arms. She passes* DAMIAN, *uncomfortable in her presence, and looms over him, refusing to go. Reluctantly he stands.*

DAMIAN: Em, it was ...

For the message to get across ... it had to be his message. The argument's so big and *strange*. If it didn't have heart in it, there's no way it would carry.

EMILY: It had my heart in it.

DAMIAN: [*shrugging*] People don't know you. Voters. G14 members. Fucking, the people in the next office. You wrote some great policy, and now it'll do what great policy does. Now it becomes action.

EMILY: But no-one will know it was me.

DAMIAN: Yeah is it really about that though?

EMILY: [*leaving*] Sexist dick ...

DAMIAN: What?!

She rounds on him.

EMILY: Ego. Pride. Those aren't just male you know. If it was a guy you fucked over, you'd expect him to be bitter. Me, you expect … understanding. 'Behind every great man' bullshit.

DAMIAN: I guess. [*Shrugging and nodding*] Yeah.

EMILY: Well—I'm bitter. I'm proud. [*Beat*] And you fucked up.

She begins exiting.

DAMIAN: It's in motion, Em. Sorry but … it's happening.

EMILY: [*stopping*] Yeah it is. We'll hibernate. But then we'll wake up. You'll wake up.

And I'll be there.

DAMIAN: What the fuck?

She looks at him and nods. She exits.

Around WARWICK, *people rally, patting his back and congratulating him as he feigns humility.*

SCENE SEVEN (H-14 MONTHS)

ALEX *stands outside the TV studio, worriedly smoking and checking her phone repeatedly.* KELLY *wanders in, dazed and covered in mud. It is a second before* ALEX *notices her but when she does, the relief is palpable. She runs to* KELLY *and stops, inspecting her shocked state.*

ALEX: Where were … ?!

They said you were in make-up, and then … you were gone? None of us knew where to. I had to read with Russell! The cops are looking for you, Kelly. They've got a helicopter out and … [*Beat*] You're covered in mud.

KELLY *nods, but is still elsewhere.*

ALEX: Kel …

KELLY: I got … lost.

I finished make-up, and I went out for a smoke. Here. I was standing right here but … my pack was empty. I thought … The corner store was just over there and /

ALEX: / You don't need to buy your own cigarettes, Kelly. Deb knows what you smoke. It's her job!

KELLY: The store was so close and I thought ... I went over. It's literally a hundred feet away.

ALEX: Kel ...

KELLY: They were ... A water truck had parked there. It had a flat so it had to stop. Up on the sidewalk, just over there. The guards were watching the crowd. You could see people circling already, eyeing off the hoses, but there were ... These three guards had their guns out while one changed the tyre so I thought: it's okay.

Someone threw a rock.

It wasn't big but he was a good shot and ... it got this guard in the eye. He starts swinging his gun round. He was blind pretty much and ... just swinging it and I'm in the middle of the road near him. He's bleeding, real angry, screaming, and ... so we all are. Lots of us, all screaming. I run for the store but the water tank's in the way and this gang—not a *gang* gang, a group—this group is heading for the release valves, for the water.

And one kid just ... swings at me. I don't know if he ... thinks I'm a guard, or *with the guard*s, or he's seen me on TV but ... He throws his hands at me. Like claws, like clawed hands. Very dry, very dusty. I can understand why he wants the water.

ALEX: Oh my god ...

KELLY: I scream ... and trip and ... roll down the embankment. Into the storm drains. Slid down the concrete and ... kind of came to rest at the bottom. Laid out on the cracked mud—the trash. All piled up down there.

And suddenly all their shouts felt ... far away. Somewhere up above me. Not about me. Nothing to do with ...

I watched the water pour over the top of the embankment. They must have got to the valves because the water, it ran in these ... webs down the concrete. Down to me. It ran around me. Me and the trash. Picked me up, with the coke bottles. The newspapers.

Then the sirens. Then the shooting. I just ... closed my eyes. Lying there with the trash. Just ... felt my buoyancy. Me and the coke bottles, all washing out to sea.

She comes to.

But no. I looked up and ... I hadn't moved. I was still right there.

Climbed up the embankment. Slipped down a bit. Climbed up again, over the top. Just over there.

I saw you. I walked over.

ALEX: You need to see a doctor right away.

KELLY: Okay.

ALEX: You need … You wait here and I'll get someone. Or you come with me, whichever you w— /

KELLY: / Okay.

ALEX: …

> ALEX *holds* KELLY. *She is still.* ALEX *holds her tightly.*

I'm so glad you didn't float away.

KELLY: Okay.

> *They stay there, caught in an embrace.*

SCENE EIGHT (H-ONE YEAR)

CASSANDRA FLORES *sits in a chair in her nursing home. Across the stage, her son* ERNESTO *speaks to her on the computer while eating breakfast at his table.* LUIS *eats at the table too, not in shot.*

ERNESTO: Mama. Morning.

CASSANDRA: Hi, my boy. Is that breakfast?

ERNESTO: Mm.

CASSANDRA: What time is it?

ERNESTO: [*shrugging*] Breakfast time.

> *He and* LUIS *laugh.* CASSANDRA *shakes her head.*

Same time as you. Always same time—I've told you over and over.

CASSANDRA: So … [*Looking at her clock*] Seven-thirty.

ERNESTO: Yup. Luis is leaving for work in a minute.

LUIS: [*leaning into the shot*] Hi, Cassandra.

CASSANDRA: Hello, handsome. [*Beat*] They didn't give *me* breakfast here …

LUIS: What? /

ERNESTO: / Are you serious? Mama, you're meant to get three me— /

CASSANDRA: / I mean okay they gave me some eggs.

> LUIS *and* ERNESTO *laugh.*

ERNESTO: Mama …
CASSANDRA: But no spices, no seasoning. Is just two eggs really breakfast?
ERNESTO: Just two eggs?
CASSANDRA: … Yeah some beans and melon. But no seasoning.

Both laugh.

LUIS: They're monsters.
CASSANDRA: They are. One girl, Masika—she's black.
ERNESTO: Mama!
CASSANDRA: She is black! Do I say she's green?
ERNESTO: You don't say anything.
CASSANDRA: Oh okay—I don't say anything. Yes, nice and silent in my old people home.

Off-camera, LUIS *shakes his head at* ERNESTO, *laughing.*

ERNESTO: You know I don't mean that.
CASSANDRA: [*silently*] Like this. Nothing.
ERNESTO: Firstly: *you are still talking*. And second: I called you! Of course I want to talk with you if I call you.

LUIS *moves beside* ERNESTO *so both are visible.*

LUIS: I'm sorry about your son, Cassandra.
CASSANDRA: You're too good for him.
LUIS: That's true. So you were saying: 'Masika is a black monster'?
ERNESTO: Jesus …
CASSANDRA: You have to go to work, darling.
ERNESTO: Yeah go to work, 'darling'.
LUIS: I've got time.
CASSANDRA: Well! She always puts away my things when I go to the bathroom. If I'm reading a book she closes it and I lose the page.
LUIS: Oh no!

ERNESTO *looks at* LUIS, *bemused.*

CASSANDRA: If I have paperwork lying round she … [*Miming*] bundles it up and everything gets confused.
ERNESTO: What 'paperwork' do you do?
CASSANDRA: I do paperwork.
ERNESTO: Like what?

CASSANDRA: Like ... crosswords.

ERNESTO: Ha! That's not paperwork, Mama.

CASSANDRA: It's on paper. I work at it. It's paperwork.

LUIS: [*to* ERNESTO] It's definitely paperwork.

CASSANDRA: See?!

ERNESTO: Yeah I do see now *thanks to both of you ...*

> *He looks at* LUIS, *who smiles innocently.*

CASSANDRA: And now! Masika says in exactly *one year today* ... I have to hibernate.

> *Both are concerned.*

LUIS: What? /

ERNESTO: / Seriously?

SCENE NINE (H-18 MONTHS AND A DAY)

EMILY *is sitting back at the date with* MARK. *He's shocked.*

MARK: What?

EMILY: Well ... it has to be that way.

MARK: Yeah but! Everything has—what do you call it?—an opt-out clause. You can't *force* people to hibernate.

EMILY: Well ... yeah you can. And also: you have to. If *everyone* agrees to this self-imposed surrender, you can't have some people who refuse and ... get to do whatever.

MARK: But it's not self-imposed. It's imposed. If your policy goes ahead, if this shitty boss of yours likes what you wrote ... It's a dictatorship.

EMILY: It's not!

MARK: You're literally dictating. He is. Everyone is *sent* to sleep.

EMILY: So they can wake up again! And wake up ... millions more times. It's to save everyone. I know the science and ... it makes sense.

MARK: Fine. But it still fucks off some pretty big human rules, Em.

EMILY: *Human rules* are the reason we're in this shit! We have *ruled* over every species. We have *ruled* over the planet. We've *ruled* over each other. And everyone is hurting *because* of those rules.

> *He goes to say something, then shrugs.*

What?

MARK: I don't know. I don't know if I'd make the choice. I just don't know.

EMILY: Well … it's not up to you.

MARK: Yeah I get what you're saying.

EMILY: No I mean: Physically. It's not up to you.

MARK: … What?

EMILY: It's a gas. 54E-501E is a gas. It's synthesised to be compatible only with human biology. It doesn't affect animals. Or plants—it only affects us. [*Beat*] But it affects all of us.

MARK *is shocked into silence and* EMILY *softens.*

There can't be an opt-out clause, Mark. Us opting out of shit (out of taking responsibility for shit) is the problem. It only works 'cause for one year we can't voice an objection. The Earth decides what happens next. We just wake up in it.

MARK: I just …

He shakes his head and both sit in silence.

EMILY: So I'm guessing no second date.

MARK: [*seriously*] Don't give him the document, Emily. Your boss. Don't start this. Don't even … put it in their minds.

Beat.

EMILY: I will.

Quietly he stands and puts some money on the table.

MARK: Too many people will die.

She holds his gaze.

EMILY: Too many people have.

He exits and she drinks a big drink.

SCENE TEN (H-ONE YEAR)

CASSANDRA *continues speaking,* ERNESTO *and* LUIS *listen anxiously.*

CASSANDRA: Masika says it's only one year—that we all do this hibernating for. Like it's nothing important. But … she is twenty-one. I am seventy-one. A year is … It's different for me.

Silence.

ERNESTO: I'm coming to visit this weekend. Both of us are.

LUIS *nods.*

CASSANDRA: Good.

ERNESTO: I love you, Mama.

CASSANDRA: I love you too, my boy.

SCENE ELEVEN (H-ONE WEEK)

ALEX *sits at the news desk, Kelly's seat conspicuously empty beside her. She is serious, stoic.*

ALEX: One week.

One week is the time we have, before *one year* begins. It will be a year of silence. Of *human* silence—the world … will make as much noise as it wants.

From midday today, Article Fifty-Eight applies worldwide. As of 12pm Greenwich Mean Time, all non-essential services cease and the three Ps are given full focus. Preparation, Protection, Provision. If you do not work in a green-flag industry, then you are free to … [*Beat*] ha … to take the week off.

That was meant to be a joke. On the auto-cue, it says it. How I should deliver it.

No. This is serious. What we're doing is serious but *why we're doing it* is serious too. This is about us having a better world. This is about us having *a* world. One for our children. One for your children. Wherever you may be watching.

In seven days, an anaesthetic gas will land upon you. It contains two hydrofluorocarbons. It contains one chlorofluorocarbon. It contains nitrous oxide.

She points at the screen and looks angrily to the side at her producer.

Again, I am not making this a joke. Turn this off. [*Listening*] I know. Turn it off.

The autocue stopped, ALEX *speaks more informally.*

This gas will be combined with the other elements of 54E-501E.

And it *will* send you to sleep.

If you are pregnant, you will stay pregnant. When you wake in a year's time, so does your future child. One hundred and thirty species of mammal use what's called 'embryonic diapause': bears when they hibernate, seals, wallabies. And luckily we're mammals too. Luckily some very clever folks in labs have identified the genes that matter, and 54E will activate them in us. It is a miracle. It is science. And it does work.

Your house must be locked—but this is because of animals. Right now, online forums are … full of people who think otherwise. Who think the threat is human. That some of us will be asleep and some will be awake.

But as the World Health Organisation says, that is not how it works. 54E makes no choices. 54E can't be bought or abused. 54E doesn't care about our politics—not mine, not yours. Its only job … is to make us sleep.

And it will.

Technology is also *not a danger*. Again, despite 'online experts' claiming otherwise, due to the use of … [*Checking her notes*] 'deep packet inspection equipment', or DPI, a total shutdown of all internet traffic is assured. It is assured, viewers. This shutdown can't be corrupted. Your bank accounts, your identity can't be erased. Your city will not be bombed.

… So long as we can make it to next week. As reported night after harrowing night, seven nations, from three continents, still refuse to accept Hibernation. They believe it's a 'godless act', that we are godless countries for agreeing to it.

But … I believe in a god. And I'm sure many of you do too. And for me … this isn't about action, godless or not. It's about inaction. It's about atoning for what we haven't done before now. And atonement …

Lost for words, she points to the heavens. Beat.

When I go to sleep, dear viewers, I will pray. And then:
I will sleep easy. I will sleep right.

She nods to her producer and the broadcast ends.

SCENE TWELVE (H-ONE DAY)

Slowly, all begin pushing furniture into new formations, fashioning beds from various pieces.

AZUBUIKE *and* CHIDERA *lie down, side by side.*

CHIDERA: I can't believe they went to sleep.
AZUBUIKE: It's like any other night for them. They don't really know.
CHIDERA: Well they asked why they were dressed. And about the shoes.
AZUBUIKE: They will sleep … a normal sleep. The gas will land on them in their dreams. They will dream a longer dream but …
CHIDERA: But we never really know how long a dream is anyway.
AZUBUIKE: Exactly. And then … they will wake up.

> *Both smile at each other, anxious but masking it.*

CHIDERA: One year.
AZUBUIKE: One year.

> *They continue watching each other.*

> WARWICK *lies down surrounded by his family, content.*

> DAMIAN *sorts paperwork, neatens his desk and switches off a lamp. He sits in the darkness.*

> KELLY *and* ALEX *scull wine and kiss, laughing and drunk and liberated and happy.*

> MARK *sits on the edge of his bed, a bottle of pills in his hand, and considers what to do.*

> CASSANDRA *stays sitting in her chair and pulls a blanket up to her chin. She closes her eyes.*

> ERNESTO *climbs into* LUIS *'arms.*

LUIS: Don't hog the bed.

> *Both laugh.*

ERNESTO: One year.
LUIS: One year.

> *They continue watching each other.*

JEONG has just completed the train track and readies a locomotive. SANG enters.

SANG: Come on, kiddo. We're all off to bed.

JEONG: Even you and Mama?

SANG: Yeah.

JEONG: But it's light.

SANG: Well, we're all having an early night.

> *She watches him.*

What?

JEONG: It's Hibernation.

> *Beat. SANG nods.*

SANG: Yeah.

JEONG: You didn't think I'd remember.

SANG: Kind of.

JEONG: Dad.

SANG: What?

JEONG: Can I sleep in your bed?

SANG: It'll be squishy.

JEONG: I don't mind.

SANG: [*smiling, nodding*] We don't either.

JEONG: And then tomorrow I'll be seven.

SANG: Kind of. Yeah. You'll be seven.

JEONG: So then I can walk to school with Bo-Young.

SANG: We'll see. We'll see what it's like.

JEONG: What does it feel like, Dad? Hibernating?

SANG: We don't … Mama and I don't know. But you don't need to worry—that's all you need to know. [*Beat*] You gonna set it off when we wake up?

JEONG: In a year? No—that'd be stupid.

SANG: That would be stupid, you're right.

> *Considering, JEONG sets the locomotive off and it journeys along the vast rail network, the tracks navigating the space and weaving between furniture and people, as ten bells chime. While this occurs, JEONG climbs into a bed between two invisible parents.*

Finally the train's journey ends. In that same instant, all except SANG *collapse into sleep.*

SCENE THIRTEEN (H)

SANG *tucks everyone in, arranging them so they sleep soundly. As he does, he speaks.*

SANG: Every door to every home is fortified. Everyone without a home lies on a cot in some church or another, great rows of metal bunks lined up side by side by side.

Every window has a curtain. Every light on every grid on every shore, switches off. Every fire is extinguished. Every plane is grounded. Every factory sighs.

Every zoo is unlocked. Every tiger walks, where every tiger chooses.

Every wave still rolls. Every cloud still breaks.

Lightning strikes a steeple and a building bursts into flame and a hundred and twenty-two people burn like string. No-one stirs, not even those on fire.

Every road is just a black ribbon.

Every baby is not born.

Every seed germinates, except for those which don't. Every shoot reaches for the sunlight. Every bud opens. Every fruit falls. Every seed germinates, except for those which don't.

Every animal is at war. Every animal is at peace.

A pack of wolves sniffs the air and finds a cottage that isn't well secured and takes a door off its hinges and eats a family. It takes apart a family and every wolf is full.

Every lover loves with their eyes closed.

Every child continues to grow older.

Every old person who would have died dies. Some who would have lived die too.

Every wave still rolls. Every forest encroaches. Every weak building crumbles. Every strong building stands.

Everyone with a bunker tries to hide from the gas. Everyone with a bunker is found by the gas.

Everyone breathes in. Everyone breathes out.

Every dream is dreamt. Every nightmare is unending. Every muscle relaxes. Every appointment is missed.

Every hour is still an hour. Every day is still a day.

With everyone tucked in, SANG *lies down beside* JEONG *and sleeps also. His voice continues.*

[*Voiceover*] Every tractor sits idle. Every harvest rots. Every harvest grows.

A roof blows off a community centre and everyone is covered in snow, still as angels, white as china. Many who lie with their faces up suffocate to death. Many with their faces to the side survive. No-one minds.

Every crocodile climbs out of the sewers. Every insect pollinates every plant. Every swarm finds your house. Every swarm finds my house.

Every month says hello. Every month says goodbye.

Every day of one calendar year passes.

Everyone sleeps.

All do, except for one.

END OF ACT ONE

ACT TWO

PETE *is cooking beans in a small pot over the flames of a fireplace in an affluent living room. He drinks red wine and reads a book.*

A floorboard creaks and he spins around, dropping the book and glass on the carpet, tipping the bottle and brandishing a shotgun.

MAGGIE *stands there, unarmed. The two stare at each other for a long time as the wine soaks into the carpet, unnoticed.*

PETE: No fucking way …

> *He lowers the gun.*

MAGGIE: I saw firelight. In that window. Thought something had gone up. Just checking no-one was burnt.

PETE: How are you here?

MAGGIE: Same as you, I guess. But I didn't think …

PETE: Me neither. After eleven months you think you're the only o /

MAGGIE: / Yeah.

> *An awkward pause.* PETE *laughs.*

What?

PETE: I planned what I'd say. If I saw someone. But … I've forgotten it. Whatever it was. What do we say?

MAGGIE: Don't know. [*Noticing the weapon*] You found guns.

PETE: Police station, couple of blocks away. They had it locked up, where they keep them.

MAGGIE: The armoury.

PETE: Oh yeah. But I used cars. Three cars. Knocked through the side wall eventually.

MAGGIE: I think I heard that? Back in Autumn?

> PETE *nods.*

It was a quiet day but I heard the wall. Thought it was just a building collapsing at first. But then I heard the engine. I ran away—the other way. Back then I didn't want to imagine other people.

PETE: No.

MAGGIE: Wanted it just to be me. Then I told myself I imagined it.

PETE: We tell ourselves things.

MAGGIE *nods.*

You said you came up here to save people—in case they were on fire.

MAGGIE: Wanted to make sure no-one was.

PETE: That's good. You must be a good person.

MAGGIE: [*shrugging*] I steal things too. I've stolen ... ha ... so much stuff. Put it all in my flat. Figure if I save some lives, maybe it balances.

PETE: It definitely would. A human life against stuff. It's not even the same.

MAGGIE: You should see my flat ...

They both laugh.

He looks down at the bottle's mess, is unfazed and leaves it pooling. He gets another bottle, fills two more glasses, drags a couch over to beside the fire, and sits back down in his chair. Considering, she sits on the couch and drinks also. He waves.

PETE: Pete.

MAGGIE *waves back.*

MAGGIE: Maggie. So you've been awake the whole time?

PETE: Mm. My housemate and me, we heard the warning sirens. And we counted down the hour from then. And yeah, we said goodbye. I put the cat outside. Set the metal bar across the back of the door. Checked the fridge was empty. [*Laughing*] All seemed so ... domestic. Just ... normal. Then I lay down in bed, looked at the ceiling. And then there were the ten bells, the last ten seconds. And I closed my eyes. And the last one rang out and ...

MAGGIE: Nothing.

PETE: It didn't work. It hadn't worked. I got up, went to ... laugh with my housemate about it. 'Fucking government—even this thing they can't do right.'

MAGGIE: But they're asleep.

Beat.

PETE: They seem fine. Nothing's wrong but ...

MAGGIE: You.

PETE: I'd done it wrong. So I lay down again.

MAGGIE: Me too.

PETE: Tried to sleep. Finally fell asleep. Finally did it. Thought I had.

MAGGIE: But then you wake up. You've just had, a normal sleep. *You're* acting normal—*everything else* is ... tipped sideways.

> *She lies down on the couch, staring up at the ceiling. He watches her, intrigued.*

I stood at my front window. Looked out at all the other front windows.

PETE: Same.

MAGGIE: Wondering if there are other people awake behind those curtains. But ... I could tell there weren't.

PETE: How?

MAGGIE: The houses ... [*Shrugging*] looked asleep. The street, looked asleep. Everything.

PETE: It's true. [*Beat*] Do you have someone? In bed—at your flat?

MAGGIE: Just stolen things. [*Smiling*] Lots and lots of stolen things.

PETE: [*laughing*] It's ridiculous!

MAGGIE: What is?

PETE: Like ... what are you even gonna do with it all afterwards? If you wanna be rich you can just ... break into cash registers, or safes. ATMs. But how does someone ... *fence* stuff? How will you sell it all later on?

MAGGIE: I thought like, a pawn shop?

> *She laughs and sits up.*

No! That's not even true. I actually haven't thought of ... anything.

PETE: What?!

MAGGIE: I've just ... got it all! Anything expensive. Just ... sitting in my flat.

> *He's laughing.*

It's actually fucking annoying. Most of the rooms I can't even move round in now 'cause of ... chandeliers.

PETE: Chandeliers!

MAGGIE: And paintings. Vases.

PETE: Do you even know about them?!

MAGGIE: What?

PETE: Vases. Like, what ones are expensive. Or collectible. Which ones to actually steal?

MAGGIE: … Nup.

They laugh. It's nice. They calm.

PETE: Thanks.

MAGGIE: You too. You can do a lot of things alone but, hard to laugh alone. I don't mean quietly, to yourself, but. Proper laugh.

PETE: Nice laugh to go with our nice six-hundred buck wine.

MAGGIE: Really?!

PETE: I looked it up.

MAGGIE: Have you got the internet?! /

PETE: / Books. [*Points to the fallen book*] Like, wine books. These guys are collectors or something. I've been reading up on what they have—it's just crazy.

MAGGIE: How'd you find them?

PETE: Breaking into different posh houses.

MAGGIE: Me too. Are they … ?

Pointing up.

PETE: Yup.

MAGGIE: [*smiling*] Did you shut their door, so you don't disturb them?

PETE: It's weird isn't it? Eleven months and it still doesn't make sense …

Silence.

MAGGIE: Do you go home at night?

PETE: [*nodding*] Leave my gun at the door. Climb into bed. Sleep. Wake up. Wake up without anyone else waking up … Go round to my parents' once a week—make sure they've got their blankets on.

MAGGIE: 54E controls temperature. They won't feel the col /

PETE: / I know. It just feels right.

She nods. Silence.

MAGGIE: I tend to stay away from people. Let them all sleep. Just pretend they're not there.

PETE: Yeah?

MAGGIE: I'm pretty solitary anyway. In the normal world. And ... it's nice to see everything happening without me. Without us. I like to climb to the top of that crane, on King William.

PETE: I've been up there!

MAGGIE: ... Oh that feels weird.

PETE: Sorry.

MAGGIE: Not your fault. [*Beat*] I sit way up, in the booth, 'bout once a month. Watch everything ... change. The dog packs, prowling in the mall. How the zoo animals go down to the Torrens now—all the fights there by the water, the blood in the water. All the new families. [*Beat*] I was up in the booth when the big South Terrace fire happened in August.

PETE: God that was huge! Two city blocks just ... So many people ...

MAGGIE: Mm.

> *Beat.*

PETE: It *is* okay though. Not the deaths—that's not okay. But ... the fact people *can* die. Or live. Or dream, or not dream. Or be eaten by wolves.

MAGGIE: Or never know anything happened ...

PETE: Or wake up and ... find all their vases missing?

MAGGIE: Their cheap, shitty vases and just ... have no idea why?

> *Both smile.*

PETE: Did you see the Parklands? After the fire—where all the ash landed. It's gonna be a forest now, 'cause of that. All these new buds. The start of a real living, healthy forest. [*Beat*] Everything that's happening—it's what should be happening.

MAGGIE: Then ... why are we awake, Pete?

> *Silence. He shrugs, then leans forward and pours her more wine. She watches, bemused.*

You trying to get me drunk?

> *He shrugs again.*

Oh god ...

PETE: What?!

MAGGIE: How old are you? Thirty-two?

PETE: I am exactly thirty-two—well done. And what, you're ... late twenties?

MAGGIE: [*feigning offence*] Um I'm *twenty-seven*! Still in the *first half, of* the latter half, *of* my twenties. 'Late twenties' ...

PETE: [*laughing*] Well for what it's worth, you're the youngest woman I've met in a while.

MAGGIE: Ha.

PETE: And ... And you know what this is too. You're experiencing this too. No-one else is, not as far as I know. The houses are asleep, the streets are asleep—like you said. [*Beat*] But you're not. And I'm not. I don't know what that means but ... It means something. It has to.

She considers this. Then considers him. Then they kiss. Silence.

I've been missing that.

MAGGIE: Me too. [*Beat*] I think we're animals.

PETE: What?

MAGGIE: You and me. I think we're more animal than human so it didn't work on us. I'm a solitary animal. And you're a pack animal. But we're still animals. My parents ... [*Getting very serious*] They were horses.

He laughs.

And yours? Tell me they were human.

PETE: [*smiling and shrugging*] I can't. I'm adopted.

MAGGIE: [*nodding*] Horses too then.

He laughs.

Do you like oats?

PETE: I do.

MAGGIE: Sugar cubes?

PETE: Oh probably more than anything.

MAGGIE: There we go. [*Smiling*] You have nice eyes, Pete.

PETE: Thanks.

MAGGIE: You have nice eyes.

She watches him.

And a nice wife.

Beat. PETE *draws back from her.*

Nice eyes. Nice wife. And a nice, new, pair of lungs.

PETE: …

MAGGIE: That's what did it. Isn't it?

> *He watches her, and nods. She patiently—button by button—opens her top.*

The gas is ingested and it … latches onto lungs. Fibrous organic human lungs. That's why we sleep, and the animals don't. Except these lungs …

> *She opens her top, revealing a large scar on her torso.*

They were made in a lab. Nice clean synthetic lungs, to replace dirty cancerous ones. And they're wonderful. And they keep me alive.

But they're not human. The gas knows they're not human.

> *She walks over and methodically unbuttons his shirt. Still in shock, he lets her.*

I went to the hospital. After I worked out why I was still awake. You knew too, didn't you—straight away?

PETE: Of course.

MAGGIE: I went to the hospital. I was lonely, and I went there and I broke in and I read the records. You went looking for guns—I went looking for you. But you're not a smoker with dirty, cancerous lungs.

> *She opens his shirt, a great many scars revealed. She is shocked and he looks at her looking.*

PETE: Car accident.

MAGGIE: [*nodding*] A car accident.

PETE: They cut me out of the car. Helen wasn't with me, thank god. I was going to Port Augusta for work and … some fuckhead cleaned me up. And then they cleaned me up, sewed me up, filled me with new bits. I've got more than you—lungs, kidneys, liver—all made. All invented in a lab somewhere. But yeah, it's the lungs that kept me awake, like you said. Clever of you to go looking.

> *Silence.*

MAGGIE: There's just the two of us. I went through all the files and it's still rare enough that we're it. I mean, in other cities yeah there's more but … we're all that's walking round here.

PETE: Wow.

MAGGIE: I watch you sometimes. Since I got your address, I go to your house and watch you from a place I broke into across the road.

PETE: I never noticed you.

MAGGIE: Story of my life.

> *Both laugh quietly.*

I see you feed your cat. [*Beat*] I see you stroke Helen's hair. See you talk to her. I can't hear you but … I see it. It's really nice.

> *Beat. He rebuttons his shirt.*

PETE: When I … After they saved me, when I was sitting up again, walking round again. Feeling it all inside me, these new parts filling me, just coming to terms with that.

[*Tapping his heart*] They didn't replace it. They kept it there, the original one. That bit was okay.

But it wasn't okay? It had lost its memory. [*Touching his head*] Not this memory.

[*Touching his heart*] This one.

I talk to Helen … to learn the words again. And the feeling that goes with the words again. It was there before the crash and then … I lost it.

> *He shakes his head, shocked at his own admission. She nods and then watches the fire.*

MAGGIE: I wasn't up in the crane—the day of the fire.

I'd only been using my car to get around. Not like you, not swapping them, crashing them into walls—I'm very boring. I like just driving mine. A small way of feeling like things are normal, normal days when I just drive round in my shitty old car.

But … the petrol stations are all empty, 'cause the government ordered that, for Hibernation. So one of the things I do is, whenever I find petrol in a car—just a random one on the street—I siphon it. I fill jerrycans with petrol and … I store it all. Store it in the one spot, so there's a big supply waiting for me whenever I need, like my own petrol station.

And there's this b— There *was* this big empty carpark, in front of a block of units, on South Terrace. It had a roof and …

He watches her, concerned.

It was just in a good place, a handy place, for me to park the car. Fill up. So I just kept stocking petrol there. More and more of it, more and more of these cans. I didn't think about it. I just ... did it. And then ...

I don't know what happened? I don't know if it was lightning or ... or some friction with the metal, the cans. If a can tipped over and spilt. I don't know.

But I heard the explosion and ... Well you know how big the explosion was.

Silence. He sits beside her on the couch, covering her with a blanket that lies over the couch.

I knew straight away what had happened and I drove there, in my shitty old car.

The whole side of the units ... was alight. These loud flames, these explosions, and then ... All these windows. Row after row of windows and ... They were all silent. Every flat, silent. Every sleeping person, inside every flat. Silent.

Beat.

The fire hadn't got to the front yet. And I broke a window—I climbed in, and I went ... just to the first bedroom I could see. And there was a man and a woman. He was too heavy so I picked her up. And I tipped her out the window. And then I found a teenager, in the next room, and I tipped him out too. Then I pulled them both to the footpath, this sleeping mum and son. I pull them to safety— and then I turn round. I go back in, further down the corridor and ... I break into another place, another flat. And I drag three people out of there. Drag them to the footpath, leave them lying with their neighbours. And then I did it two more times—six more people in those next two flats. And that's eleven people.

And then the smoke ... There was a lot of smoke but ...

She is crying, struggling to make sense of it.

I thought I heard a baby? Even though I didn't, you know. Even though I know there wasn't one—or if there was it wouldn't have been crying but ... I heard one. It doesn't matter that there wasn't one—I heard one.

So I went back in.

But the smoke was … It was all just smoke. And there was no baby. Not even the noise of a baby. Just smoke. And I was vomiting. Even my new wonderful synthetic lungs couldn't handle that much smoke. So I went back outside, just made it outside, to my eleven people on the footpath. To my eleven saved people, that would maybe, *maybe* balance out all the other people. And …

The animals had come to see the fire.

PETE *is crying.*

I thought it might've scared them off. Thought that's how nature works but … [*Shrugging*] Turns out it works different. Maybe they smelled the … I don't know why they were there. But they were.

And the dogs. And the hyenas. And the lions. And the crows.

They had found my eleven people.

Beat.

They found them all.

Silence. She smiles sadly and wipes her eyes. She looks at PETE *and sees his tears.*

Why are you crying?

PETE: You have … I don't have my memories, Maggie. And you have too many. [*Beat*] I don't know which is worse.

They watch each other. And then kiss. And then kiss again. Silence.

MAGGIE: What were you planning to do?

PETE: What do you mean?

MAGGIE: At the end of the year. When everyone wakes up again?

PETE: [*shrugging*] Climb back into bed. Throw away the gun. Lock the cat out. Put the bar on the door. Change back into my old clothes. Lie back down beside Helen. Wake up again, with her, pretend to wake up like she wakes up and … Start making memories. New ones.

She nods.

MAGGIE: Don't.

PETE: What?

MAGGIE: You think … You think you're awake, because of lungs, Pete. But I think you're awake … So you could find me. So I could find you.

PETE: You think the whole world went to sleep for a year. You think *everything stopped* … so we can fall in love?

MAGGIE: [*shrugging*] There are crazier things.

PETE: No—there aren't.

MAGGIE: Yes. There are.

> *He laughs.*

PETE: What would I … ? Where will she think I've gone?

MAGGIE: She will think, you have vanished.

PETE: And … Where *would I go*?

MAGGIE: I have a home—it's full of stolen things. Things that might not be valuable. But … that I've taken. Because I like them.

PETE: Ha.

> *She touches his chest.*

MAGGIE: This needs filling.

> *She takes his hand and mirrors the image.*

This needs emptying.

> *They kiss. Silence.*

> *They sit in the silence.*

SCENE FIFTEEN (H: NO TIME. PLUS A DAY)

MAGGIE *sits waiting outside at a pub table, before* PETE *emerges with two stubbies.*

PETE: Know how long it took to get served in there?

MAGGIE: [*laughing*] Terrible joke.

PETE: All the taps were off so I got stubbies, sorry. Warm stubbies too.

MAGGIE: [*raising a cheers*] To a year of free drinks.

PETE: [*shaking his head*] I can't do it—not here. Left a twenty on the bar for Kev, beside all the money from my other visits.

MAGGIE: Should I go in and count how much there is?

PETE: … Please don't.

They smile and drink in contented silence.

MAGGIE: This feels ... normal. I mean, yeah we have guns in case dogs come. And the streets are messy. And a million people are asleep around us. But it feels ... like a date.

PETE: It's weirding me out to be honest.

MAGGIE: [*laughing*] What, more than Hibernation? More than *the packs of wild animals*?

PETE: Seriously! Doing this is ... I feel very strange, Maggie.

MAGGIE: How long's it been?

PETE: Nine years. It's nine years since I took Helen on a first date.

MAGGIE: Well you must be good at them—a house, a marriage.

PETE *looks guilty.*

Sorry I said ... I don't mean to make you uncomfortable.

PETE: But it is. It's not your fault—it just ... [*Shrugging*] Is.

MAGGIE: The world's done something really odd. The rules of the world are broken. You can't ... It doesn't work to hold yourself to them.

PETE: But the world'll wake up, soon, in three weeks. The world wakes up and ... the rules apply again. Yeah? If you were married, you're back to being married. If you have a life together ... You still have it.

MAGGIE: If you live alone, and feel alone, nearly all the time ...

PETE: I didn't mean to /

MAGGIE: / Hm.

The pair drink in silence. She points across the road.

That building over there, that business—it used to just be a homewares shop. It sold incense and ... bowls and stuff? It didn't used to be full of birds. There used to be a window there and ... nature stayed outside. But nature got in. The window broke. The birds found it. They start nesting in there. The eggs hatch. More birds are born. Now it's all birds.

And yeah, maybe the owner cleans it when she wakes up. Maybe she works really hard. Fumigates it all. And it goes back to being a homewares shop.

But for a year ... [*Smiling and drinking*] It *was* full of birds.

Silence.

You felt something when we kissed. You felt something last night at my flat. And I'm not saying it's as big as what being married feels like.

But it is a thing you felt too. One doesn't cancel the other. [*Beat*] They both exist.

PETE: How do you know? You don't know.

MAGGIE: I do though. 'Cause we all do. We all feel more than one thing. We're all good. And we're all not. That's just ... what being human is.

PETE: I can't leave her.

MAGGIE: Maybe. But ... now you can't leave me either. Not anymore.

Beat. He stares at the shop.

PETE: It's just ... Messy.

This city—it used to be clean, you know. Then it got sick, the whole world got sick. So it went to sleep—to heal. That's what it needed. And while it was asleep ... It got messy.

He drains his drink, exasperated.

I like you. And that's messy. I wanna not like you. I wanna ... fall asleep and wake up and ... It's all a dream.

But that's not gonna happen now.

MAGGIE: I'm sorry.

PETE: No. You're not—not really. And I know 'cause ... a part of me isn't either. Like, it feels shit, yeah. But it also feels ...

Beat.

After the ... [*Gesturing to his injured and rebuilt body*] The walking, the talking, they came back pretty easy. The holding a cup. Remembering names. Shaving. The functioning—yeah. But not the feeling.

They even congratulate you—when you register sensation. An ice-cube on the back of the hand, and you flinch a bit, and they say: 'See?! You're feeling again!'

... But you're not.

The whole world went to sleep, Maggie ... [*Laughing*] And I barely even noticed.

Beat.

And then you walk in. To see if something's on fire. And you're
hurting—and I'm numb. And we joke. We kiss.
And I wake up. For real this time. Suddenly. Annoyingly.

He looks at her.

And maybe you stole that. From Helen. Maybe her eyes would've
opened, in three weeks, and she would've looked at me. Helen
would've kissed me. And her kiss would've done that to me.
... But now I'll never find out.

She looks at him.

MAGGIE: You could go back and see. You could wait ... three weeks
and see.

PETE: [*nodding*] ... Yeah.
But I would know. Maggie.
I would always know ... That the shop was full of birds.

Accepting, he rises and extends a hand.

Can I show you something?

She rises. Hand in hand, they walk offstage.

SCENE SIXTEEN: H (NO TIME. PLUS AN HOUR)

PETE *and* MAGGIE *lie in long grass, which blows languidly around
them. The dappled light of a canopy glints upon them. They stare up.*

PETE: I only thought to come here last week. I'd driven past the oval so
many times, and it's so big but almost ... too big to notice. Plus it
was locked. I had to break into the security office first, and there's a
lockbox in there, and it had a key.
I used to come here with Dad to watch the tests. For years, since
I was young. Still do sometimes 'cept ... [*Smiling*] We don't sit
under the scoreboard anymore. Up in the Members now. And I
thought: what'd it be like—to stand at the crease. Stare out at the
seats. Maybe I wanted to feel powerful. Or the opposite—feel like a
kid. Do what kid-me always dreamed of doing. So I broke in.

MAGGIE: But this is what it is now.

PETE: The tarp must have blown off a while back and the roof is open
so ... just got left to the elements. Winter rains were heavy so it

got a good soak. And spring's hot anyway but in here … it's like a biodome.

He references the skies.

And then they found it.

MAGGIE: All those birds … All those bats, hanging asleep in the rafters. All these bees—a million, billion bees all round us. Anything that could get through the roof, it did.

PETE: And the birds shit down seeds. Seeds land in the soil. The bees move the pollen round. And eventually …

MAGGIE: A whole giant garden …

And no animals. And no people—not even sleeping people. Just the air. And the bees. And things growing.

PETE: And you. And me. Somehow … we get all this.

She lays her head upon him. He decides.

And I don't want it to end. Even when it ends … I don't want it to end.

She smiles. The birds pass in a grand murmuration.

MAGGIE: And so … It doesn't.

At peace, decided, they close their eyes and fall into a sleep.

As they do, all others wake.

Blackout.

END OF ACT TWO

ACT THREE

SCENE SEVENTEEN (H+20 DAYS)

The set has changed. The world has changed.

WARWICK *stands at a hastily convened town hall meeting.* DAMIAN *stands behind him, as supportive advisor.* MARK, *wearing a press badge, addresses* WARWICK, *the mood combative.*

WARWICK: We are saying /

MARK: / Because early reports are proposing eighty thousand deat— /

WARWICK: / We are *saying*—if you'll let me finish please, Mark—that every death is a tragedy. The ideal number of victims in 2030 was of course zero.

MARK: So you were expecting zero deaths? That's what your estimates were suggesting?

WARWICK: I didn't say that. I said that was the wish. The reality— as with every reality—is of course different. If you really want to know about our modelling /

MARK: / We do, Minister. Australia does.

WARWICK: Well then *Australia* will be happy to know, Mark, that projections were higher. Far higher.

MARK: And yet despite these 'far higher' projections, you persisted with Hibernation? /

WARWICK: / But if you hold *those figures* up against our other set of projections! Which was doing nothing! Which was doing what some people, on some other sides of the aisle, and some people in the media, would have had us do ... Well then you're really looking at a scary number. Then we are talking deaths edging close to a million. And that's here—in Australia. *Globally*, the price of doing nothing in 2030—of expecting nothing, and being ready for nothing when it did come ... would have been catastrophic.

MARK: So just to clarify—is entire families dying in fires *not* catastrophic, Minister?

    Beat.

WARWICK: What are you doing, Mark?

MARK: I'm asking a question on behalf of my newspaper. On behalf of its readership. They want to know if /

WARWICK: / Have you researched this line of questioning?

DAMIAN begins talking quietly to WARWICK *but he ignores him.*

MARK: My colleagues and I are simply putting ques /

WARWICK: / Edna Grace Grant …

DAMIAN tries to intervene.

Give me a minute, Damian. Edna Grant … is my mother. She is a resident of Saint Carmel's Aged Care Facility.

Cameras begin flashing.

Saint Carmel's is located on South Terrace in Adelaide.

MARK: Minister, we haven't been made aware of /

WARWICK: / One of the worst hit sites of environmental disaster—or possibly foul play we're still not quite sure—to have occurred /

DAMIAN: / The minister will have to leave it there so /

WARWICK: / *To have occurred* during Hibernation. Edna Grant is eighty-six years old. She is unable to walk. She is a loving mother to four children, and grandmother /

MARK: / Warwick I'm honestly sorry about that ques /

WARWICK: / And grandmother to nine beautiful grandchildren.

DAMIAN: Okay, Minister.

WARWICK: And you'll notice I say *is*, rather than *was*, Mark. Because … Because the site's still being investigated. And I am hoping … There is a corner of me which is hoping … that something has occurred, which is not the thing *we all think* has occurred. That … I don't know—I don't know what I'm hoping for. But … You do, don't ya? You hold onto something. Something small. No matter how small.

DAMIAN: If everybody could please /

WARWICK: / So when I say every death is a tragedy, Mark, you mouthy little shit /

DAMIAN: / Okay, Minister!

WARWICK: Then … That's what I mean. *That's* what I am talking about.

He walks off, leaving DAMIAN *at the podium.*

DAMIAN: Um Mark ... If you want to meet up with me in a minute, we can ... talk about this further. Thanks, everyone.

SCENE EIGHTEEN (H+TWO MONTHS)

CASSANDRA *sits at a table with* ERNESTO—*they live together now. He prepares breakfast while she speaks to us.*

CASSANDRA: The birds ... are mind-blowing. Their numbers have grown so vast and they live on everything. And in everything. Any window that broke, any wall that fell down. The birds came in there and they made their homes.

All the dairy cows are dead. Billions of them. They weren't made for this, for time without us. Within *one week*—all dead. Either they mooed for water that did not come, until they were just bones. Or the dogs found them.

Dogs are everywhere. They had to be let out of the houses, before we went to sleep. Which is good because ... [*Shrugging*] they would have eaten us. They love us, sure. But you know they would have done it. And quickly. So they prowl the streets of our towns and cities, first alone, then in packs. Their jaws are wide and merciless. They are never nice. It is like we were never friends.

The oceans love us being gone. They're new things now. Coral is such beautiful colours, more than we thought we remembered. Fish fight each other for space. Pow pow pow! Of course we're trawling them again. It's only made us greedier because ... we are what we are. But now they have a good head-start. We will fuck it all up again, sure. But in the meantime we can eat like kings and queens. And we do.

The cities look sad up high and wonderful down low. Tall buildings, they turned out to be weak. Their steel rusted. Their windows broke. Their bits and pieces have all gone missing. But down below ...

The subways of so many cities they filled with water, straight away. And then the streets did. And now if your city once held an underground, or a Metro, or a Subte, your roadways are waterways. And the buildings that sit beside them are not ready for this. They grow weaker by the day and every so often one falls. And where it lands it smashes through the concrete. And there the water pools again, and new tributaries form.

I really think water might be everything. Maybe evolution is playing a game, spinning the clock backwards, slowly returning us all to the water. Our legs might go. Our toes might web. Our gills might form once more. We might breathe again, without breathing. This is a year.

ERNESTO: Breakfast is ready, Mama.

He gets a bib and puts it on her, then gently touches her chin and she opens her mouth. He begins spooning in food and she chews, rhythmically but vacantly.

LUIS *enters, adjusting a suit, and sits. He tucks into breakfast.*

LUIS: Morning, Cassandra. You think she's having a good day?

ERNESTO: Sure. Aren't you, Mama?

He continues feeding her, dabbing her mouth clean.

What's today?

LUIS: Talking with Australians.

ERNESTO: Oh yeah?

LUIS: There were two there who didn't go to sleep—they think they came here.

ERNESTO: They're here now?

LUIS: Or came through here, we don't know.

ERNESTO: How many didn't go to sleep, do they think?

LUIS: [*shrugging*] Couple of hundred. Mostly Western, mostly in cities. Wherever the surgery's more common.

ERNESTO: The lung surgery.

LUIS: Mm. Eight Latino, but we caught them already.

ERNESTO: That's quick.

LUIS: It wasn't hard. They got braver, and stupider the longer it went on. Forgot they leave DNA. Most of them just went home afterwards— thought it'd be okay. It's not okay.

ERNESTO: Did they do really bad things?

LUIS: … You don't want to know.

ERNESTO: I do!

LUIS: You say that but. You never do. When I tell you the stuff I see, you say you wish you didn't know.

ERNESTO: This is different though. Us all in Hibernation and them being able to ...

He makes an expansive gesture and LUIS *shakes his head.*

LUIS: It's not different. People are people. Good ones are good. Fucked ones are fucked. Sorry, Cassandra. You give people a whole year, a whole city ... [*Beat*] They did the things we expected them to do.

ERNESTO: That's all you're giving me?

LUIS: [*smiling*] Good breakfast.

ERNESTO: Fuck you. Sorry, Mama.

ERNESTO *finishes feeding her and begins eating his own.*

Have you been practicing your ... [*accented*] English words?

LUIS: They give me a translator.

ERNESTO: You don't need it. You're good.

LUIS: The stuff we're talking about's pretty complex. My shitty English won't cut it.

ERNESTO: I could translate. My English is great—way better than yours. Then *they* could tell me what the sleepwalkers did.

LUIS: [*shaking his head*] 'We are bound by an international code of silence.'

ERNESTO: Fucking cops.

LUIS: Yup.

ERNESTO: One big happy family.

LUIS: Just ... so happy.

Both keep eating.

ERNESTO: You hear the shooting last night?

LUIS: Don't worry about it.

ERNESTO: You don't worry about it. Me and Mama sitting at home all day, knowing that four floors below us they're /

LUIS: / We have locks. We have a gun.

ERNESTO: You take the gun to work with you.

LUIS: You want me to bring you back a gun?

ERNESTO: I didn't say that /

LUIS: / I can get you a gun. We can have one ea /

ERNESTO: / I don't want a fucking gun, Luis. [*Beat*] Sorry, Mama.

LUIS: Sorry, Cassandra.

Beat. He pauses his meal.

People are scared. They don't have much. What they had, they lost. Or ate. Or shared. Like I said, people are people. The ones with guns—they were probably doing ... bad shit beforehand anyway.

ERNESTO: [*nodding*] And they live four floors below us.

LUIS: [*nodding*] And now we know about them. We're rounding so many up, honey—you wouldn't believe. Hibernation ... It brought the plants out of hiding. And the fuckheads out of hiding too.

ERNESTO: Ha.

LUIS: It's all visible now. We keep what's good. And we clean up the other stuff.

ERNESTO: Fucking cops ...

LUIS: Just keeping your city safe, Sir.

He rises and kisses ERNESTO'*s head.*

Thanks for breakfast. [*Holstering his gun*] Don't open the door.

ERNESTO: Love you too.

LUIS *exits. Silence.* ERNESTO *looks to* CASSANDRA.

Whose turn to wash up?

He laughs to himself and clears the plates.

SCENE NINETEEN (H+SIX MONTHS)

AZUBUIKE *sits, watching still water. Finally, the surface breaks and* CHIDERA *rises, taking a deep breath. She wades stoically out.*

AZUBUIKE: No sign?

She collapses onto the footpath beside him, breathing calming breaths. He begins to rise.

My turn.

CHIDERA: [*stopping him*] I'll go again. Just ... give me a minute.

AZUBUIKE: You're tired.

CHIDERA: We're both tired. Lie with me for a bit.

AZUBUIKE: I'll just do one more.

CHIDERA: Azubuike ... He's not going anywhere.

AZUBUIKE *pauses, resigns himself to this logic, and lies down beside* CHIDERA. *They stare up.*

So many birds.

AZUBUIKE: The number there was always meant to be. We have gone all these years—all these centuries—thinking we knew birds, not realising what we are missing out on, what they can look like in that number. Look at them …

Together, they watch the flocks which pass overhead.

CHIDERA: School opens next week.

AZUBUIKE: Already?

CHIDERA: That's what they say. Or … some kind of school. Dr Nweke said he'll get a class running at his house until proper rooms are found.

AZUBUIKE: But they don't have any laptops anymore. Or books. Or /

CHIDERA: / He has enough things. He'll find a way to make it work.

AZUBUIKE: He's a good man.

CHIDERA: Yeah. [*Concerned*] Obuya … He always walks to school with Ohon.

AZUBUIKE: He can … He will walk with the neighbours. Or we will walk him. And soon he can walk by himself.

CHIDERA: The water though—crossing it.

AZUBUIKE: We can go over the bridge, up by the park.

CHIDERA: He needs Ohon's help with maths. Ohon always makes time to look at /

AZUBUIKE: / Obuya will be fine. Or he won't. He can fail at maths and … I won't care. He can be a mechanic and I won't care. He can be a drug addict, I won't care. [*Beat*] If he is not lying at the bottom of a river … I don't care.

They both watch the water.

CHIDERA: Why did he go in?

AZUBUIKE: The boys I spoke with—the ones with him … They say they saw a turtle. A really large turtle. Just … swimming through the city.

CHIDERA: A turtle?

AZUBUIKE: From the zoo maybe. Or … from the sea—maybe from a thousand miles away but … [*Shrugging*] It found its way here, while we were all asleep. And he dove in to get it. The others wouldn't— they were scared.

But he did.

Silence.

CHIDERA: How do you catch a turtle?

AZUBUIKE: I have no fucking idea. I'm sure he didn't either.

CHIDERA: Did hunger make him dive in?

AZUBUIKE: [*nodding*] But not his own. He wanted to feed us all with the turtle, that's what the boys said. [*Sighing. Smiling*] Never came up.

CHIDERA *shakes her head. She looks at her husband.*

CHIDERA: Does Ohon swim with the turtle now, Azubuike? Here or … a thousand miles away?

AZUBUIKE: No. [*Beat*] Ohon … is dead. And Aisha … is dead.

He stares at the water.

But Obuya … is alive. And next week, we will walk him to school, okay?

CHIDERA: [*nodding*] Okay.

He rises, but she places her hand on his shoulder, pushing him down and rising in his place.

I have my breath back now.

AZUBUIKE: Are you sure?

She nods, and wades back in.

SCENE TWENTY (H+TWO YEARS)

PETE *and* MAGGIE *are seen entering Seoul, separately and ostensibly for different reasons. They do not acknowledge one another and, when called, go to different customs counters.*

1: What is the nature of your visit to Korea?

PETE: A conference.

2: What is the nature of your visit to Korea?

MAGGIE: Holiday. Um, pleasure. I'm on holiday.

2: First time?

MAGGIE: Yes.

1: What kind?

PETE: Sorry?

1: What kind of conference?

MAGGIE: I got a cheap flight—think they're trying to … get everyone travelling again.

2: Mm.

MAGGIE: I mean, I wanted to come anyway! I've always wanted to. It's beautiful.

2: 'It's beautiful.' So you've been here before?

MAGGIE: [*shaking her head*] I *heard* it's beautiful. First time.

PETE: Hydroelectric. Energy. It's an annual conference and … Korea's hosting.

1: You are a businessman?

PETE: [*shaking his head*] Consultant. I set up hydro schemes in Queensland. In Australia. And yeah … just talking to your guys for a week.

1: Our guys?

PETE: I mean the equivalent peo /

1: / You have paperwork? An invitation?

PETE: Sure. [*Beginning to get it out*] It's on my phone, is that oka …

The CUSTOMS OFFICIAL *curtly gestures for him to hand it over and he does.*

2: You are travelling alone?

MAGGIE: Yes.

2: You always travel alone?

MAGGIE: Um … no. Sometimes I've … travelled with other people. I mean, it depends whe /

1: / You are travelling alone?

PETE: Yes.

1: Where are you staying?

PETE: [*pointing to the screen*] It's … there on the phone. I can't pronounce it sorry.

2: Have you travelled since Hibernation?

MAGGIE: Not out of Australia. I went to Tasmania—my stepdad lives in Ulverstone.

2: I have been to Tasmania.

MAGGIE: Oh? Right. Great.

2: It is very beautiful.

MAGGIE: Yeah. Yes, absolutely.

1: Have you travelled since Hibernation?

PETE: Couple of times.

1: For conferences?

PETE: Mm. Cheap flights. Think they're trying to get everyone travelling agai /

1: / Welcome to Seoul. Enjoy your conference.

PETE: Oh great. Thanks—I will.

2: Welcome to Seoul.

MAGGIE: Thank you. Hope you get back to Tasmania one day.

2: It is a dream of mine.

MAGGIE: Oh. That's lovely. Goodbye.

> MAGGIE *and* PETE *leave their* OFFICIALS *and re-enter a crowd. They look at each other and share a small smile. Then realising the circumstances, she pointedly looks away and, remembering, he does too.*

SCENE TWENTY-ONE (H+FOUR YEARS)

EMILY *sits in one of a circle of chairs,* KELLY *and* ALEX *in two more.* KELLY *rises.*

KELLY: Friends, this is … We're very lucky. Our guest tonight … She is the architect! It was her that first imagined what 2030 would be. And it was her … who received no credit for it.

> EMILY *smiles humbly.*

No praise.

But that is changing! Because the world is changing. The world has changed. And now she's crossed that world … (we are so honoured, Emily) … to speak with us—her American friends. I should say, her American fans.

> *All laugh politely.* KELLY *raises her hands apologetically.*

And we aren't many. But we are listening. Please—Emily Metcalfe, everyone.

> KELLY *sits,* ALEX *patting her knee proudly.* EMILY *rises and people clap.*

EMILY: Thank you. Really, Kelly—and Alex. You two bringing this group together is … amazing. It's great to see you all and … thanks for the help in getting me over to your beautiful country. Now …

She gathers herself.

There's an irony in who we are. Who this group is, and who its sibling groups are—its brothers and sisters in every city, every town, across the globe—I hear about more every day. And the irony's this: When the push for civil rights here, in your country, began—and I mean when it really … grabbed the minds and hearts of people, even the white people—*its voice* was Martin Luther King. Eloquent and loud and sure, a reverend's voice.

But *its body*—its heart—was Rosa Parks. Quiet. And normal. And acting … only because there was no choice. And the people saw that. And they realised *they* had no choice either.

When the Raj was toppled, it was this … small bald man—this smiling patient man, the exact opposite of any general we can imagine—who told people to hold on. To wait it out. To know that a better thing was coming. A better way of being.

When the hippies needed symbols, for the peace they were … trying to express but couldn't, they chose two lovers—a famous musician, an infamous artist—and that couple stayed in bed. They didn't go off to any fight. They stayed where they were and demanded, *quietly*, that the world change. That it be better than it was.

When the tanks had to be stopped in Tiananmen … *the people lay down.*

Beat.

And the tanks kept rolling … But the cameras did too.

When a famous man had to show the injustice he felt about the Vietnam War, he didn't raise his fists—and how paradoxical is that? He was a boxer! Raising fists was what he did. It was why the people loved him. [*Beat*] But he set aside those fists. *He set aside that love.* He was hated. And unarmed. And he sat in jail.

And that is it! That's the line, the one same line, that runs through last century's great upheavals. Muhammed Ali *sat.* Gandhi and his followers *sat.* Rosa Parks *sat.* John and Yoko *lay down*—and they

became symbols. The students in Tiananmen Square *lay down* ...
And they became martyrs.

All of them—all these acts which ... ripple. Which happened
then, but which we know about now. And *understand now*, as ... as
re-imaginings of the world. As schisms which in some small way
shifted the world ...

Their key ingredient ... was stillness. They did nothing. And it
meant everything.

Because stillness is potent. Stillness is powerful. Stillness—and this
is the simple, perfect irony in our language—stillness *is* a movement.

And there's nothing as still ... There's no time when we're more
defenceless—and so also when we're *more brave* ...

She smiles.

Than sleep.

Hibernation is the greatest act, the greatest fuck you. Hibernation
is our movement—the twenty-first century's movement. We will lie
down for this. We will proselytise for this.

Because ... to become a knight, you don't rush towards great
armies. *You kneel* ... in front of a single sword.

To pledge eternal love ... You do not cross the world for
someone. *You wait* ... at an altar for them.

Four years ago, brothers and sisters, *we pledged our love* for
a planet. By bowing to it. By telling it, it was bigger and we were
smaller. We put our life in its hands.

And we were repaid! We were repaid a thousand times over.
The skies tell us that! The seas tell us that! The fact we're here—so
many of us still alive when really we shouldn't be ... It tells us that!
And that is why ...

Hibernation must return. Nine years of us doing as we please
can only be balanced ... by one year of submission. One in ten must
not be for us.

'Cause since the Industrial Revolution, brothers and sisters ...
Since the first factory roared into life ... Since the first smokestack
coughed, the first car rolled off the first conveyor belt ...

We have been making our beds. And now ...

Now we must sleep in them.

Finished, EMILY *sits and* KELLY *emphatically shakes her hand, as the listeners cheer, a chant of 'one in ten' building.*

SCENE TWENTY-TWO (H+SIX YEARS)

ERNESTO *sits at his table, Cassandra's chair empty,* LUIS *also absent. He dials on a laptop.*

On her bed, Chidera's laptop rings and she enters from another room, answering. Both wave.

ERNESTO: Hi, Chidera.

CHIDERA: Morning, Ernesto. Are you well?

ERNESTO: Sure. And you?

CHIDERA: I was cleaning my son Obuya's room—he is ... [*Laughing*] really messy.

ERNESTO: So get him to clean it.

CHIDERA: We have had that chat maybe ... ten thousand times?

ERNESTO: No luck yet?

CHIDERA: Ten thousand and one—that will do it.

ERNESTO: [*laughing*] The magic number.

CHIDERA: You have children?

ERNESTO: No. Just my husband and I.

> *Beat.*

CHIDERA: You are a gay man.

ERNESTO: [*smiling*] Yes. You alright?

CHIDERA: Once I would have not been alright. Now ... Now everything is new.

ERNESTO: Well, that's one good outcome I guess.

CHIDERA: I think so too.

> *Beat.*

ERNESTO: So! /

CHIDERA: / So!

> *They laugh.*

I was going to ask ... [*Shrugging*] Why are we talking today?

ERNESTO: Okay. I ... My mother, Cassandra, she died, er ... five years ago now.

CHIDERA: I'm sorry.

ERNESTO: Thank you. And at first I thought—okay, she was old. She lived a life. My papa was dead long before her. So that's that. You accept it.

CHIDERA: But you didn't accept it?

ERNESTO: Not over time. Over time I got … angrier. Hibernation … It took years off her. Like, yes she lived a life. But she could have lived a longer one. Another ten, maybe fifteen years of my mama existing. And everyone says: 'well that's the price to pay'. But *they* didn't pay it, the ones who say that. She paid it—an old lady, in a poor country. These are the ones who pay.

I'm sorry to ask but—you lost a parent too?

CHIDERA: A son.

ERNESTO: Oh god.

CHIDERA: I had two—the messy one, and him. And also a daughter but her death was … a whole other tragedy. I do not blame Hibernation for her. But … I wish to blame it for something. For someone. Ohon he was called. He still is called.

ERNESTO: Of course.

CHIDERA: Hibernation turned our city—do you know where Lagos is?

ERNESTO: … In my mind, yes. On a map … [*Smiling*] Sorry.

CHIDERA: That's okay. It's exactly my point. *The rules for Hibernation* were made in Washington, in Shanghai. In Berlin. And we can point to them on a map. But *the price for Hibernation*—it was paid in Lagos. And no-one knows where to find me. To find me and say sorry to me.

ERNESTO: …

CHIDERA: Hibernation turned my city into rivers—and my son, Ohon … he dived into one. For a turtle he had seen. Or heard about. Or maybe only imagined, I don't know, and … He drowned.

ERNESTO: That's so awful, Chidera. But you know that already.

CHIDERA: …

ERNESTO: My mama Cassandra—after Hibernation she was … mostly silent—not all of her woke up. But one thing she *did say* was: water might be everything. That evolution was playing a game, spinning the clock backwards. Our legs would go. Our toes would web. Our gills would form once more. We'd breathe again, without breathing. That's what she kind of rambled about, at the end.

Sorry if I'm offending you?

CHIDERA: Oh … [*Staring off*] Everything about Ohon offends me, Ernesto. Everything anyone says. To make me feel better. Or to blame him. Or praise him.

    The fact he is not here, offends me. The fact we are all meant to celebrate the thing that killed him, offends me.

    Silence. He nods.

ERNESTO: I feel the same with Mama. [*Beat. Cheering up*] And that's why we're talking!

CHIDERA: Yes! We are a 'global grassroots movement'.

    Both laugh.

ERNESTO: Sounds ridiculous, doesn't it?

CHIDERA: [*smiling*] I do not wish to be in a movement—I am just one sad mother. But I worry Hibernation will return. And then there will be *more sad mothers* without sons. [*Beat*] And more sad sons, without mothers.

    So! I add my name to an algorithm, it connects me with a stranger who feels the same. And we talk. And a conversation grows. And one day maybe it is so loud that governments hear it. That Washington and Shanghai and Berlin hear it.

ERNESTO: That's all we can do, Chidera. Small voices.

    Both of their computers ring.

    It's another person. Are you happy for me to add them or /

CHIDERA: / Sure. My husband is watching the football. I'm not busy.

ERNESTO: Great.

    He accepts the call and DAMIAN *appears, seated at his desk, also online.*

    Hello … Damian. This is Ernesto in Bogota. This is Chidera—she's in Lagos. How are you?

DAMIAN: Hi, mate. Yeah good. Or, you know, not so good. Thinking about what to do really.

CHIDERA: You are in good company.

DAMIAN: [*laughing*] Great. Being a bit cheeky actually—calling from work.

CHIDERA: You're not a brain surgeon are you, Damian? If you are, please … hang up now.

DAMIAN *and* ERNESTO *laugh.*

ERNESTO: Yes, Chidera!

DAMIAN: No no. I promise they won't notice I'm gone. [*Becoming serious*] Government. I work with the Australian government.

The others become a bit uncomfortable.

It's okay. I'm just here as ... me. Not running numbers or ... meeting the enemy or anything. I'm just ... second-guessing myself I s'pose. Way more than second-guessing actually—fiftieth-guessing. I've been thinking about this stuff for a while.

ERNESTO: Hibernation?

DAMIAN: Mm. I think ...

I think we made a mistake.

The other two nod and listen, none sure exactly who should speak next.

SCENE TWENTY-THREE (H+EIGHT YEARS)

MARK *and* WARWICK *are in the final throes of a fight in the middle of a pub.*

Finally MARK *admits defeat and* WARWICK *nods wearily, stumbling to a stool. After a moment,* MARK *sits beside him—both are beaten up and nursing fresh wounds.*

MARK *holds his head up, attempting to stem a nosebleed.* WARWICK *addresses the publican,* NIGEL, *who resets any upset furniture.*

WARWICK: Sorry, Nigel. Whatever we broke ... Put me down for it.

He lets out a deep breath and tends to his jaw. NIGEL *shakes his head and carries on.*

MARK: Feel better now?

WARWICK: Put your fucking head forward, Mark. Haven't you had a nosebleed before?

Embarrassed, MARK *does this and lets the blood-flow slow.*

And yeah, I do feel better. 'Cept for my jaw ... My jaw does not feel better.

MARK: Sorry about that—just got a lucky one in.

WARWICK: Too right you did. You are shit at fighting, mate.

Painfully, WARWICK *gets out cigarettes and lights one.*

NIGEL: Can't smoke in here, Warwick …

Exasperated, WARWICK *gestures to his surroundings, alluding to all the rules already broken.* NIGEL *sighs and carries on.* WARWICK *hands the pack over and* MARK *accepts it.*

WARWICK: You know you had that coming.

MARK: Probably.

WARWICK: No—you really did. That stuff you said about my mum, on live TV …

MARK: That was, fucking … eight years ago.

WARWICK: Exactly my point. Right after she died. Cunt move, mate.

MARK *lights his cigarette and nods, chastened.*

MARK: Sorry. I honestly didn't know.

WARWICK: 'S okay. It was a shitty time.

Silence.

MARK: You glad you left it? Parliament?

WARWICK: We on the record, are we?

MARK *laughs, and crosses his heart.*

Nah. They forced me out.

MARK: Really? I never heard that.

WARWICK: Oh that's good. They promised they'd keep it low-profile but … I didn't actually believe it. Nah, I was already a dead man walking by then.

MARK: 'Cause of Hibernation?

WARWICK: Mm. Hard to sell as a success—which it fucking was, ya know! But yeah, the spin was never gonna go our way. All the people still alive 'cause of us, they didn't know we saved them. And the ones who had people die—they did all the talking to you lot. So it just looks like a fucking disaster. Which I didn't help by crying about my mum on the bloody ABC.

MARK *laughs. Silence.*

It's all good. Politician me was a shit dad, shit husband. I'm a better guy now.

MARK: Well, you just beat me up so …

Both smile and sit in silence. MARK *doesn't look at* WARWICK.

Hey is that true about Emily Metcalfe?

WARWICK: Little Miss 'One in Ten'?

MARK: She's getting a lot of airtime, in a lot of countries, saying she brought Hibernation to you.

WARWICK: Yeah well—she can have it.

[*Calling out*] Nigel, get us a couple of pints would you?

Look it was a good idea—it was a great idea actually, but … [*Shrugging*] A million people have great ideas every day. And they're just too … poor. Or brown. Or … boring, for anyone to listen. She should thank me for getting it up.

MARK: Oh she does. Often. Says how she tricked you. Sold it as something to fuck the Chinese with. But how really … she used you all. A right-wing government accidentally spruiking this … humanist policy.

WARWICK: Conservatives are humans too, you dickhead.

NIGEL *brings the pints.*

Cheers.

MARK: She thinks One in Ten'll … create a new balance. Flatten out rich and poor. And you gotta admit, she's not looking wrong.

WARWICK *nods and sips his beer. Beat.*

WARWICK: You know what I do? Now I've got all this free time? A fat government pension?

MARK: I don't know—consult?

WARWICK: I hunt. I always loved hunting. Did it with my dad when we were on the farm. Even when I got to Canberra, started wearing a suit, I found a club and started shooting there. Got my kids shooting too. One of them, Nathan, he's a better shot than me.

And what Hibernation did, Mark—what *really* happened in 2030 *from my perspective* … was a whole lot of populations that'd been pretty thin on the ground, they restocked. We're talking gamebirds, wild pig, deer, the ones you'd expect a hunter to notice. But also stuff like dog numbers—how suddenly they were this huge pest, and so we introduced these urban quotas.

Now for a hunter—and particularly one who's been newly fired from his very stiff, very formal job, after fucking *years* of … sitting in an office, talking with wankers like you … I was in heaven. Absolutely lapped it up.

So yeah, good on Emily for selling it as this big eco-friendly paradise. Personally, I don't think she cares about that, think she's as much a politician as the rest of us but … Yeah, good on her anyway. She's playing the message well.

But that doesn't mean we've all got to, Mark.

He sips his beer.

You reach a point, when you're old enough, cynical enough, where you realise … You can let other people make the plays. Let them tell you what a thing means. And in the meantime you just … [*Shrugging*] Do whatever the fuck you want.

So I'll go to sleep in 2040, sure. I'll say yes to One in Ten and bunker down with everyone else.

But I won't be dreaming about … the people of Bangladesh getting another decade of clean water. I'll be dreaming … about a fucking northern white rhino, waiting for me when I wake up.

I'll be dreaming about blood.

Smiling, he finishes his pint and stands.

Write any of that in your paper, Mark, and I'll deny every fucking word.

WARWICK *puts money on the counter and waves to* NIGEL.

I'll get these.

NIGEL: Look after yourself, Warwick.

WARWICK: Cheers, Nige.

He exits.

SCENE TWENTY-FOUR (H+EIGHT YEARS AND 364 DAYS)

DAMIAN *is sleeping. He wakes and discovers* EMILY *sitting on the end of his bed. He freaks out and sits back in shock, but she gestures for him to be calm.*

DAMIAN: How the fuck did you get in here!?

EMILY: Fire escape.

DAMIAN: I don't ha ... There is no fire escape!

EMILY: Oh. Then I broke in.

DAMIAN: ...

EMILY: I said it. One day—we'd wake up. You'd wake up. And I'd be there.

DAMIAN: Yeah, I didn't think fucking *literally* ...

EMILY: Surprise.

She looks around the room.

You live in a shit flat, Damian. I thought you'd have more money—you've been in government sixteen yea /

DAMIAN: / I'm not chatting with you, Emily!

What are you even doing?! Are you gonna ... attack me? Like, are you crazy now? Do you have a weapon?

EMILY: You don't seem too scared?

DAMIAN: I'm confused! I am scared but ... at the moment I'm more confused and then once I understand yeah, then I'll probably be scared. I guess. I don't know.

EMILY *smiles and puts her hands up, begging peace.*

EMILY: It's okay. I'm not armed. I'm not crazy (I don't think). I'm not gonna attack you. But I hate you. From back then, what you did. And ... I wanted to tell you.

DAMIAN: ... Well ... you have. I acknowledge it. Fuck off.

Again she ignores him, walking to his bedside and drinking from his glass.

That's my wa—

She sighs.

EMILY: Saw they put you in charge of managing the Hibernation message this time round. Which is ironic.

DAMIAN: Why?

EMILY: 'Cause you don't want it to happen.

DAMIAN: ... How'd you know that?

EMILY: I know lots of stuff now. I'm powerful now. Not some random who 'people in the next office wouldn't know if I tried to convince them of something big'.

DAMIAN: Yeah sorry I said that.

EMILY: I did convince them. Millions of them. Billions. I have an aeroplane now. My own aeroplane. I go round meeting with heads of state and eventually …

She makes a sleeping gesture. DAMIAN *nods.*

DAMIAN: Yeah. You did it. You convinced everyone to Hibernate again.

EMILY: Not just again—not once. Lots of times. It's a cycle now, Damian. And all the shit that all the wrong leaders do …

'Cause honestly pretty much every government is led by the wrong person—I've met them and … it's not even a joke …

But now everything they do in nine years, gets judged by the planet in the tenth—with all of us fucked off to bed. And *that thing* takes no prisoners. If your systems are weak …

Then buildings fall. Then people die. And the survivors will be angry. And systems—fundamentally flawed systems—will topple. Not after the last Hibernation. Maybe not after this one.

But eventually.

She lies beside him in bed and stares at the ceiling. He doesn't stop her—he just watches her.

DAMIAN: So it's that big for you? I thought it was just … politics. You angry after what we did, trying to ruin us. But you're about changing everything. You sound angry at everything.

EMILY: I'm just angry at one person.

DAMIAN: Warwick? I mean, he's a cunt but /

EMILY: / Not Warwick.

Elsewhere onstage, MAGGIE *lies dressed on her own bed, older now, staring at the ceiling too.*

You know … You know the ones who set the big fire in Adelaide? All the people who died—Warwick's mum in her home?

DAMIAN: With the fake lungs and … They went off to South America or something?

EMILY: [*nodding*] Maggie's my sister.

DAMIAN: Seriously?

EMILY: No-one's noticed yet—we got different surnames from different dads and … I left for Canberra years ago, but yeah.

DAMIAN: I've seen her. That footage from the street, where she's pulling the bodies out. When Warwick opened the inquiry into his mum ... Jesus, I had to sit through hours of that.

EMILY: ...

DAMIAN: She doesn't ... You don't get the sense she's a bad person. She's trying to ... do the right thing. That bit when she comes out and sees the animals ...

I can still see her collapse.

EMILY: ... Yeah.

DAMIAN: Do you know where she is?

> PETE *comes into the room. He is older now too, recognisable as* SANG. *He lies beside her and strokes where her scar is. She smiles.*

EMILY: I never found her. I've always been looking. I had people whose job is looking work for me on it. Quietly.

> LUIS *triple-checks every lock on the door of his apartment. Satisfied, he lies down beside* ERNESTO. ERNESTO *holds a gun against his chest.* LUIS *smiles and holds him.*

But they lost her too. And it makes sense—I've always been ... me. Loud, sure of what I want. Usually getting it. Knowing I deserve it. Maggie's not that. She always could disappear. In crowds. On Christmas mornings. She'd be there but ... You kind of easily forget she's there.

The idea of everyone watching that footage—her and the bodies. All the people in the world with their eyes on her. It's ... [*Shaking her head*] Yeah.

DAMIAN: So ... You've set up another Hibernation, what—for her?!

> *Beat.*

EMILY: The first one made her disappear. Maybe the second one brings her back.

DAMIAN: No. No, Em. All the deaths. All the upheaval. You just want to find your sister?

EMILY: It's not about finding. It's about not losing. Too many people ... have lost too many people. For too long.

> *Silence.*

DAMIAN: I spoke with a woman once, in … Africa somewhere. On this online thing. Her son drowned. He was on a flooded street, trying to catch a turtle, to feed his family.

> AZUBUIKE *and* CHIDERA *lie in bed together, their shoes polished.*

Their city … It had all turned to water.

> CASSANDRA *swims alongside a giant turtle.*

Everything … Everything they knew, had turned to water.

> KELLY *and* ALEX *shout at each other, angry and drunk and crying and sad.*

> ALEX *storms out of the room and* KELLY *screams in frustration.*

EMILY: I think … Water's okay. Even if some people drown. I don't want them to. But if they do …

> *Beat.*

I think everything has been like me, for too long. Like you and me and Warwick.

> WARWICK *lies down surrounded by his family, content.*

Knowing what we want. Sure we deserve it. Loud.
But I think … I think it's time for us all to be like Maggie.
To disappear for a bit.

> MARK *sorts paperwork, neatens his desk and switches off the lamp. He sits in the darkness.*

To be alright with that.
The lie I told the world, is Hibernation will save us. The lie I told myself … is Maggie's coming home. But the truth is …

DAMIAN: What?

EMILY: The truth is: we don't even come into it.

> *She smiles.*

It's not about us.

> *Silence.*

How long?

DAMIAN: [*checking the bedside clock*] Ten minutes.

EMILY: Do you want me to go?

DAMIAN: Where would you get to in time?
EMILY: Nowhere.

He considers, then motions for her to get out of the bed. Saddened, she does.

He adjusts a pillow and pulls back the blanket. She smiles, removing shoes and climbing in.

They lie together.

SCENE TWENTY-FIVE (H+EIGHT YEARS, 364 DAYS, 23 HOURS AND 56 MINUTES)

PETE *and* MAGGIE *lie in bed.*

MAGGIE: It's nearly the bells.

Both shake their heads in wonder.

PETE: You ready?
MAGGIE: More than last time.

He kisses her and rises.

PETE: 'Kay. I'll go get her. Love you.
MAGGIE: Love you too.

He rises and goes to JEONG.

As they speak, the train reverses its journey, weaving along the track in reverse. Eventually the locomotive is returned to its owner, waiting patiently at JEONG's *hand.*

PETE: Come on, kiddo. We're all off to bed.
JEONG: Even you and Mama?
PETE: Yeah.
JEONG: But it's light.
PETE: Well, we're all having an early night.

She watches him.

What?
JEONG: It's Hibernation.

Beat.

PETE: [*nodding*] Yeah.

JEONG: You didn't think I'd remember.

PETE: Kind of.

JEONG: Dad.

PETE: What?

JEONG: Can I sleep in your bed?

PETE: It'll be squishy.

JEONG: I don't mind.

PETE: [*smiling, nodding*] We don't either.

JEONG: And then tomorrow I'll be seven.

PETE: Kind of. Yeah. You'll be seven.

JEONG: So then I can walk to school with Bo-Young.

PETE: We'll see. We'll see what it's like.

JEONG: What does it feel like, Dad? Hibernating?

PETE: We don't … Mama and I don't know. But you don't need to worry—that's all you need to know. [*Beat*] You gonna set it off when we wake up?

JEONG: In a year? No—that'd be stupid.

PETE: That would be stupid, you're right.

Considering, JEONG *sets the locomotive off and it journeys along the vast rail network, the tracks navigating the space and weaving between furniture and people, as ten bells chime. As this occurs,* JEONG *and* PETE *climb into bed beside* MAGGIE.

Finally the train's journey ends. In that very same instant, all collapse into sleep.

A moment passes, before PETE *and* MAGGIE *stir and sit up. They look at their sleeping daughter. Quietly they climb from bed and tuck her in.*

Then they smile at each other and, hand in hand, walk out into the sleeping world.

THE END

www.ingramcontent.com/pod-product-compliance
Lightning Source LLC
Chambersburg PA
CBHW050022090426
42734CB00021B/3376